A
POWERFUL
WOMAN

ACTIVATE YOUR POWER NOW!

BY:

JAZMIN ANDERSON

A POWERFUL WOMAN,
"Activate Your Power Now!"

ISBN: 978-0-578-83780-2

Printed in the United States of America

Motivate One

TABLE OF CONTENTS

DEDICATION

I dedicate this book to you!
You're making the Choice
To Dominate!
To Conquer!
To Prosper!
To Tap Into Your Best Self!
Your Journey Awaits!
It's time to Activate Your POWER!

INTRODUCTION

Being a woman is one thing. Embracing, accepting, and using your full potential as a female is another. Throughout the past centuries, womanhood has become associated with weakness, sacrifice, powerlessness, codependency, over-sensitivity, and over-emotionality. We now live in a society where feminine energy is not glorified but suppressed, and that demands more masculine energy in us to operate, belong, and be accepted. In other words, some will say "it's a man's world." However, we know that's not the case.

This masculine energy translates to qualities like drive, independence, aggression, arrogance, competitiveness, and confidence, which are required to succeed in today's world. These are not bad traits, and there is no denying that we need them. Indeed, they may have allowed women to become CEOs and leaders, but they have also led to us losing touch with our real power—our real magic, if you will. We've prioritized masculine over feminine energy and need to recognize the key to this puzzle: balance-- it is achieving harmony between these two types of energies.

Are you aware of the powerful and magical energy you carry within you? It's time for you to activate and awaken this immense, creative, joyful, playful, pure, and open force starting today.

A Woman's Power

You are equipped with everything you need.

Let me tell you my story, which explains why it is important for me to share this message about tapping into your inner power.

As a growing young woman, I have had some challenges with understanding and knowing the true depths of being a woman. In April 2019, my realization of not knowing the full potential of a woman hit me bigger than ever. I had just moved from my home to a new place; I gave away my furniture and left my vision boards and a lot of my things at my old residence. In my head, I guess I was starting fresh. Little did I realize I was leaving my safe place, an atmosphere I created where I could really be myself and creativity could flow, to be in a relationship. Without really knowing that I was putting everything I knew to the side, putting my goals and dreams on hold to help pursue someone else's. I was putting myself last — thinking I needed to relearn things. I was feeling like I wasn't enough. I started to feel empty so I would play that song by Tasha Cobbs "Fill Me UP." It was like I had to redefine who I was and what I wanted. Like I had to regain control of who I was and who I was created to be. I wanted to tap into my highest-self more than ever. I knew in order to do that, I had to let go of certain people and habits to protect and build my energy. I really wanted to reset myself mentally or tap into a greater power within myself. I no longer wanted to just have potential; I wanted to be powerful, assertive, significant and dominate-- the way I was created to be.

I had questions, and I wanted answers. I was pacing around the house going back and forth wondering about how to live out my purpose more, asking who am I fully? What are my capabilities? What are my strengths and weaknesses? What, as a woman, do I offer to the world, to my child, to my future spouse, but most importantly, to myself. Have you ever felt like you could almost lose yourself-- the part you did know-- the part of you that you thought you were totally in tune with?

I have always wondered what made a woman full. What makes her a woman? Is it how she dresses, her career, her finances, her outlook on life? Is it being a mother or speaking her mind? Or is she full of wisdom and possess an energy that gets people to do whatever she asks? Really though, how valuable is a woman? What is a woman designed to do? What are her "Superpowers?" What is her reason for existing? What is she equipped with? What does she possess? What makes a woman a woman? Not just any woman but a virtuous woman, a kingdom woman, a powerful woman, a woman with values & principles. These were some of the questions I was curious about.

On the journey to understand what a powerful woman is, I found myself recognizing my full capability. I interviewed powerful women, and with their perspective, in their own words, they shared views through their quotes. I, too, wanted to share my perspective so that any girl or woman would know everything she was created to do by knowing the powers she possesses inside of her and how to use them.

I researched and did a lot of introspection; I interviewed many ladies to get their insight on what a woman is equipped with. I wanted to know for myself. No one ever just told me outright. My Mom and aunties shared more about the mannerisms of how a woman should act growing up. As a woman, I needed to know more than just that. It's like I learned a lot from trial and error.

Mistake after mistake. Lesson after lesson. This time around, I had questions and wanted real answers. So, through my journey of getting the insight I needed to walk in my full power, I have put together this amazing masterpiece to help other women tap into their power and ACTIVATE IT as well.

In this book you will learn and be empowered to stand strong in your power as a woman. There will be a few questions at the end of some chapters to help you reflect on how to activate your superpower. I want you to revisit your answers whenever you need a little motivation or an extra PUSH.

It's time to use all that great potential, because you are equipped with everything you need. Now it's time to tap into your Energy, your frequency, and activate the power that is within you to dominate and impact the world.

As you read through these pages, I want you to recognize the power that lies within yourself that the creator has given you. By the end of this book. You will have the knowledge you need to activate your power and be the woman you were created to be. Remember to enjoy the journey and use your superpower.

CHAPTER 1

CREATION OF THE CREATIVE MIND

Creativity is intelligence having fun. In other words, being creative doesn't necessarily mean you are artistic or musical. It means that your brain is designed in a way that helps you solve problems, think up new ideas and have insightful moments. Creativity is a gift that some are not necessarily born with. It's a beautiful trait that through habit can be honed. With the right practice and persistence, you can rewire your brain to make the most of your inherent ability to generate original ideas and be creative.

The brain is a complex and hardworking organ. It is made up of as many as 100 billion neurons or brain cells, but only weighs 3 pounds. It is an energy intensive organ, making up around 2 percent of a person's weight but using a huge 20 percent of the body's energy. When you can manage your mind, you can manage your life. We will come back to that topic and discuss the laws of the mind.

Let's first talk about the creation of the woman's mind from when she is created.

A woman is a powerful being. The woman gives life. Every organ inside her body can create life. Everything a woman needs to create and grow a life is already inside of her. Her organs-- her womb, oxygen, the brain, eyes, body, hands, feet, bones, liver, and heart-- are all formed inside of the womb.

Your physical development starts from the inside of the womb. You begin as a fetus. Your features are created from your hair follicles all the way down to your toenails. You are a masterpiece with a light of power inside of you. After you are born and as you grow, your life continues outside of the womb. You are curious about what you see, what you smell, what you hear, taste and touch. Your senses can be curious all at once. You want to know who you are; how did you get here; where you are; what was before you; what were you created to do; how you are supposed to live; what language you are supposed to speak; and how did you get your name? You have question after question. Your mind is constantly thinking and taking in information at the same time.

You are looking at your surroundings and trying to get an understanding in your mind. The creative mind starts to awaken. Your brain is naturally seeking knowledge to grasp. You create your own atmosphere, language, ideas-- that you feel are correct. But you are still curious about what your mind was created to do. What information were you programmed to give and receive? You realize that you are unique; you are different; and you have a wild imagination. You can see things before they happen. Yet sometimes you can forget who you are, what you were called to do, and where your power lies. Has this woman ever been you?

Creativity is a big part in being a woman. Whatever you're doing, it should bring added value and creativity to your perspective and your expertise. Your brain is made up of two sides: Left (Masculine), Right (Feminine). Located in the left side of the brain is the masculine force. It is the part of us that is assertive, logical, analytical, doing, controlling, aggressive, striving, projecting, hard, organizing, rushing, thrusting, and always pushing us to survive,. The right side of the brain is feminine. It is the creative, delicate, intuitive, nurturing, receptive, tender, surrendering, synthesizing, integrating, soft, feeling, and the part of us that "knows" without explanation (intuition). Its roots reach deep into the heart. The feminine helps us to "be." It's not just your genetics that define how good you are at creative thinking. Your experience, your style of thinking, and even your emotions also play a role in being creative. Your level of creativity and your mood are linked. I'm sure you have heard how being positive is good for you. It is good for your health. It is good for your social relationships. It is also good for your creativity. Happiness is the best emotion for creative thinking. Being relaxed or serene is not as good as happiness. Neither is being sad or anxious. This means that you don't just need to be in a positive mood to harness your creativity; you need positive energy. This is one of the biggest reasons why it's important to be conscious about what you are putting in your mind from the time you wake up to the time you go to sleep. In the mornings I like to listen to classical music, gospel, uplifting content, or my powerful woman playlist. I also read a motivational message and I look at my vision and lifestyle board. After that, I go over my schedule and look at what needs to get accomplished for the day. I like to see my vision daily and visualize it already taking place. Every day, I complete at least one thing for my vision. I have a weekly goal of five things that should get completed. I don't like to make too big of a list because I don't want to overwhelm myself. I also take a moment and congratulate myself for accomplishing each goal. It's healthy that you encourage and motivate yourself. Give yourself a pat on the back and say, "you did that. I'm proud of you, let's continue turning those dreams into our reality."

Having a creative space at home or your workplace makes it easier to tap into your creative mind. Designate an area where you can create and have your accomplishments and positive sticky notes around you. Your thoughts influence your actions.

The best way to build a creative mind is through practice. Below are some creative pursuits, choose which one works for you and do them regularly-- daily if you can. The more you flex your creative muscle, the more your mind will naturally innovate. Creative practice reduces stress and improves problem solving. Here are some suggestions that can help you tap into your creative thinking:

1. Mindful observation (This is our ability to create. It begins with observing the world around us; how we perceive our surroundings, and our environment fuels our creativity. Start by noticing and appreciating the details of your surroundings.) Look around you.

2. Change your environment (Your surroundings may be zapping your inspiration. One easy method to rekindle your creativity is to try changing your environment. Switch up the atmosphere. Try packing up your laptop and find a restaurant, cafe or even a park where you can work for a while. In addition, set up your workspace in a way that is conducive to being creative. Make sure you have a dedicated space where you can create, and only create, whether in a work office or in your home.)

3. Take a "creative" walk (We all know exercise is good for your creative thinking as well. Simply getting up and going for a walk will improve brain function and boost your creativity. Walking benefits creative brainstorming and enhanced divergent or unconventional thinking.)

4. Recharge your curiosity (Creativity thrives on curiosity. Our ability to wonder, to dig into something and search for answers, ignites our creativity by asking questions. Start living a curiosity-driven life. What piques your interest? Delve into it, examine and research it. See where your line of thinking takes you. You may see that you thrive on the process of discovery. The more you know, the more your mind is awakened, and the more you want to learn. This will open your mind to new possibilities.)

5. Practice creating. Even for the most creative and innovative people, about 10% of their work is natural talent and 90% is labor. You can cultivate your creativity by challenging yourself to create every day, in whatever way speaks to you-whether it is writing, editing, drawing, photography, painting, dancing, singing, or creating music. Push pass your initial ideas. We often focus on concepts we already know. Don't self-edit but give yourself freedom to go in different directions. Let your ideas flow, then look at them more critically. Creativity is a process that takes time and effort.

6. Build a creative portfolio that inspires you (Reflect on what inspires you to be your best, creative self.)

Also, you can ask yourself these questions:

- What helps you tap into your innovative thoughts and ideas?

  ....

- What are the first things you listen to or watch during the day?

  ....

- What's the first thing you eat? (What you eat should fuel you and give you energy.)

  ....

- Are there certain blogs, books, or videos that shake up your thinking and spur ideas?

  ....

- Are there activities that always seem to relax your mind and help you look at things in an unconventional way-- such as journal writing, meditating, or going for a run?

  ....

- What are the first words you speak when you wake up?
- Who is someone you admire or look up to?

  ....

You should put together a creative portfolio of things that help you tap into your creative energy and original thinking. If you enjoy drawing, try keeping a sketch pad or doodle book. If you like to write, keep a notepad handy to jot down random thoughts. Make time to write every day. If you find inspiration in nature, try collecting small items from your time outside, or take pictures of scenes you find stimulating or exhilarating. Whatever you find interesting, motivating, and inspiring, use it to help rewire your brain and boost your creativity daily. Place these objects and positive sayings in your creative space that is designated to just creating.

If you win in your mind, you will win in life.

Let's talk about three important laws for the mind.

1. Your mind needs to **focus.** (You need to focus on something in your future or a task. Two parts of your mind are your *memory* and your *imagination.*) Your memory replays the past and your imagination pre-plays your future. Focus on the Newness ahead.

   The picture in your mind controls your behavior. You will always act like the person you think you are.

2. Your mind needs **instruction**. Speak to your thoughts to control your thinking. Your mind is an emotional magnet searching for information to verify your opinion or to escape the present pain it's feeling. Your mind is always looking for information-- it's desperate for new knowledge. Your mind requires instruction.

3. Your mind needs a **hero**. You need someone who inspires you, that's a champion. You need an example. Your hero decides your energy, endurance, and experiences. Research or think about one person who has succeeded where you want to succeed, anyone who has mastered or conquered what you want to conquer.

Those three laws help me to prosper in my life. Now you can apply them to help reposition your thoughts to stay on track, when needed.

"Your mind is a garden. Your thoughts are the seeds, you can either grow flowers or grow weeds."- **Osho**

Watch what kind of seeds you put in your mind. Think about it: Everything starts with your mind: what you are thinking is exactly what you will do.

"Watch your thoughts, they become words. Watch your words, they become actions. Watch your actions and they become habits. Watch your habits, they become your character. Watch your character, it becomes your destiny." -**Lao Tzu.**

The brain is powerful. It's fully within your power to practice your creative thinking. To turn your creative thinking process into a habit, make sure you revisit the suggestions and laws we just went over, because what you are putting in your brain will definitely come out. Let's put in our brain good ideas, good books, shows, podcasts, movies, food, and music. Things that stimulate your brain to grow where you are learning new things daily. Initially, that's how you will evolve and be more creative. The mind is a powerful source. Use it wisely. Now that you have been informed...

Your creativity has been unlocked!

POWERFUL WOMAN FACTS

Mae West

Mae West was 38 when she was offered a contract by Paramount Pictures in 1932, and by 1935 she was the second-highest paid person

Mae once stated, "You only live once, but if you do it right, once is enough," was saying that she had enough success to last several lifetimes. In addition to being a superstar actress, she wrote nine of her 13 films, and is known equally for her bon mots and intelligence as she is for her buxom beauty.

Ada Lovelace

Though she's often called the world's first computer programmer, Ada Lovelace lived almost 100 years before the first "computer" was even built. A brilliant mathematician, she wrote the world's first algorithm for a computing machine and predicted that someday computers would be used for composing music and producing graphics.

CHAPTER 2

THE SOURCE OF WISE CHOICES

Every decision should be based on your intellect/knowledge and understanding. A wise woman makes wise choices because she uses reasoning and logic, not her emotions. The primary difference between logic and reason is that reason is subject to your personal opinion, whereas logic is an actual science that follows clearly defined rules and tests for critical thinking. Logic also seeks tangible, visible, or audible proof of a sound thought process by reasoning.

Who is the wise woman?

She's clear in her decisions.

Within her lies the universe. Her spirituality keeps her aligned and connected with life. She is multi-faceted and has many different characters, personalities and titles depending on the circumstances and situation. They all make up who she is.

The source of her wisdom comes from her belief. She is confident in who she is. The source is the heart and mind.

The heart is the person. Everything belongs to the heart. Everything depends on the heart. Because the heart is personality, moods, goodness, and meanness. It is courage or fear and anger. I tell you again, for us, the heart is everything.

It's very important to control your anger and emotions so you can hear yourself and make wise choices. Not just react. A lot of times people act now and think about it later. In my early 20s, I made a lot of choices based on my emotions. I have not always made the best choices, but based on that experience, I have used wisdom to make better ones. For example, because of my emotions, I chose to be in a relationship with a bad guy instead of the good guy. I know I'm not the only woman who has made a choice like that. Well, with the good guy, I saw how my life would be clear as day and I knew he loved me; with the bad guy, I didn't know what the future was with him. It was blurry, but I knew that I loved him, and I was curious to see what life would be with him. Based on emotions, I chose the bad guy and the unknown, instead of using logic. The good guy had a career, stable income, loved me and I could see my future as clear as day. The bad guy was not good for me, he was virtually abusive, looked like he had it all together but didn't. At the end of that heartbreak, I learned that I want to be able to envision a positive, productive life with anyone I choose to be in a relationship with. If I can't see that I don't give them any attention. So, I learned from that experience. I had to look at the positives and be discerning about what I did and didn't like in my past relationship. Overall, every person you meet has something you're supposed to learn from them and take that information with you along your journey. It's all about how you look at the situation. There's a blessing and a lesson in everything.

My sister is working on her doctorate degree and is having a few challenges, I mentioned to her that each level of your life you will be tested. It's like in school you must take a test before you can go to the next level. The teacher must see if you learned the information before they give you a passing grade, and if you don't they hold you back. I told her the same way you pass those tests in the academic world is the same way you must pass the test in your personal life. Every person you encounter is a teacher. From the strangers you meet to the people with whom you choose to have relationships. Everyone is teaching you something, whether you realize it or not. I was telling her to embrace the moments of life right now, it's a gift. As long as you're living you have the choice to be better, do better, and want better for yourself-- in the now! Every day you make the choice. I said look at those past relationships that didn't work, focus on what you learned, what you liked about that person and what you didn't. Add those things you liked to your mental note of who you want to attract. The things you didn't like, add those to the list of what you won't allow. Now you can peep through a pattern of certain behaviors. I believe people should focus more on the fact that they got a chance to experience a person. Every teacher you had you didn't like, and some I'm sure you couldn't stand, but the ultimate question is did you get what you were supposed to learn? That situation was put there to give you the knowledge you need on your journey. Then I told her, "you know when you have those good teachers, you want to stay in their class forever and wish other teachers could be just like them. However, you have outgrown that class and it's time for you to go to the next level." The key thing is, look at what people are teaching you and let it advance you. Everything can better you if you choose it to.

One thing that always comes to mind when I make a choice is," Your Life is a Result of Your Choices". I remember hearing someone say that, and it stuck with me-- because it was true. I looked at my life and realized everything leading to this present moment stemmed from a choice I made. It helped me be accountable for my thoughts and actions, and to make better choices in my life. My results were the reality of my life. Deep, huh? To be honest, you can look at someone's life and see the choices they have made because of their reality. Let me tell you the good news: you can start today and make better choices that will bring the results you want in your life, right now.

Even in making great choices, life will always have challenges, but it's how we handle them that keeps us moving forward. The secret is to push forward even if it's a baby step-- even when it hurts or doesn't feel good. Push, little by little.

Focus on finding solutions as much as possible. You are always in control. Some women find themselves emotionally attached to the point where it can cause mental illness. If you can't control your mind, you will have something or someone else controlling you. Everyone has a breaking point; you must control your thoughts and your emotions. Below, I have listed some ways that helped me get through challenging situations. I know they will also help you to be mentally strong,.

Become Emotionally and Mentally Strong

1) Identify your weaknesses and learn from them
2) Never let stereotypes break your spirit
3) Take control of your life and be whatever you need to be, now

4) Realize that nothing is too ambitious if you just do your best and plan for success

5) Expect love and friendships to hurt sometimes but keep pushing forward and heal at your own pace

6) You don't have to be strong all the time; you must vent, breathe, and let your emotions out by journaling or talking to someone

7) Don't let others call you weak just because of the circumstance, you might have had a weak moment but you're not weak

8) Let go when you know it's becoming too much, it's not worth your peace or happiness

9) Be kind to yourself because you deserve it; you must take care of yourself before you can help anyone else

10) Refuse to be silenced, use your voice, tell your story

11) Hang out with people who love you and who you know are on your team

12) Challenge yourself with a small goal, then attempt an even larger one

13) Don't keep going back to things that have hurt you

14) Play positive music and videos

15) Focus on what you want and how you want to be treated

16) Forgive yourself, love on yourself

17) Face what's bothering you and ask yourself, why is this upsetting me? Breathe and see how you can go about it better the next time

18) Be productive

19) Work-Out and eat something healthy

20) Pamper yourself and dress up for you today

Emotional and mental strength is what makes women more powerful and gives them the ability to adapt to almost any environment. Everyone is not lucky enough to learn the skills that can be harnessed from these unique strengths. Some women learn after mistakes have been made, and from choices they can't take back.

You can control your temper and actions. Sometimes, to calm your nerves, you might need to take a deep breath in and exhale-- and that's okay. Take that moment to pause and think about the next step or what could happen if you make this choice. Ask yourself, "Is this the right choice?" In doing so, you can make wise choices that bring value to your life.

Choose which voice you will listen to... CHOOSE WISELY!

GOD'S VOICE	OTHER VOICES
Leads you	Drives you
Reassures you	Scares you
Refreshes you	Drains you
Calms you	Worries you
Comforts you	Aggravates you
Strengthens you	Questions you
Heals you	Hurts you
Encourages you	Discourages you
Gives you hope	Steals your peace and joy

Every day you can choose to get better or be dull and plain. What I mean is that either you are getting better or getting worse. Some people might think they are just standing still. You have the free will to choose the path you want to go down. Every day, every single choice you make brings future results. You have the power to make the shift in the way you think and decide what will be the result. You hold the power!

What choices have you made today that are going to better you? What or who do you choose to listen to?

Remember, the present (right now) is a gift.

Moving forward and learning from the past, what is your big picture dream?

....

Are you choosing to be happy and push forward no matter what?

....

I want you to choose you. I want you to choose the best in life, period-- because that's what you deserve. Before you can give or share your best with the world, you must give yourself your best, first.

My confession for you is: "Your power to make wise choices has been unlocked."

Lifestyle & Vision Board Project:

I think it's important and necessary that everyone has a *vision and a lifestyle board*. It's time to manifest what you want in your life-- to see more clearly the life you want and have. On your vision board, you will put your vision for what you want to create. For example, a business idea, business creation, the plan for it and pictures of the logo, building, van, billboard, how many people you want to work there, and how you envision it. Even put a picture of you on the board. Whatever your vision is, I want you to create a board with just your vision. Then I want you to put together a lifestyle board. On this board, I want you to put pictures of how you see your future life. For example, you will have photos of how you will dress, what you will drive, and what house you will live in. When you travel, will it be by jet or plane, where do you want to visit, will you be in the community at non-profit events, volunteering? Whatever you want your lifestyle to be, I want you to put that on a lifestyle board. Once you complete those two, I want you to hang them up somewhere you can look at them every day. I do this every year, sometimes twice a year. It really works in my life, so I wanted to share this secret. It also helps me stay positive and make wise choices based on my vision and my desire for a prosperous lifestyle. If you choose to share yours when you finish, use #pwvisionboard or #pwlifestyleboard or Tag: @powerfulwomanbook on social media to share with other ladies.

POWERFUL WOMAN FACTS

Eve

Eve was the first woman on earth, first wife and the first mother. She is known as the "Mother of All the Living." And even though these are rather remarkable accomplishments, little else is known about Eve. Like many noteworthy mothers, even though Eve's accomplishments were significant, they were mostly overlooked. We learn from Eve that women share in God's image.

Feminine qualities are part of the character of God. God's purpose for creation could not be fulfilled without the equal participation of "womankind."

Rhonda Byre

Rhonda Byre is listed among Time Magazine's 100 people who shape the world. Her book "The Secret" has re-popularized the spiritual belief in the Law of Attraction and positive thinking.

CHAPTER 3

A VIRTUOUS WOMAN
IS STABLE

A virtuous woman is a woman after God's own heart. This woman stands firm in her convictions and is not easily swayed by whichever way the wind blows. She is consistent, stable, and hard working. Her confidence is found in the Lord, and she keeps the company of those who add value to her life.

This is not because she considers herself better, but because she values her peace and the things that she lets into her mind. Her guidance and wisdom come from the Lord and she seeks His way and not her own.

This woman practices the law of kindness when she speaks, and her faith is strong in the Lord. In Proverbs: 31:10 it says," Who can find a virtuous woman? For her worth is far above rubies." She is rare and hard to find.

A virtuous woman is what we all have probably heard about but never really knew about. No one ever really taught us exactly how to be. We may have just read the verses and said wow that's what I want to aim to be, a woman of valor. As you read this notable passage from the Bible, remember you are still an extraordinary woman in-the-making.

Proverbs:31:10-31

The Price of a Virtuous Woman
10 who can find a virtuous woman? For her price is far above rubies. 11 The heart of her husband doth safely trust in her, so that he shall have no need of spoil. 12 She will do him good and not evil all the days of her life. 13 She seeketh wool, and flax and worth willingly with her hands. 14 She is like the merchant's ships: she bringeth her food from afar.

A Virtuous Woman Cares for Her Family
15 She riseth also while it is yet night, and giveth meat to her household, and a portion to her maidens. 16 She considerate a field and buys it: with the fruit of her hands she planters a vineyard. 17 She girth her loins with strength and strengtheneth her arms. 18 She perceiveth that her merchandise is good; her candle goeth not out by night. 19 She layeth her hands to the spindle, and her hands hold the distaff.

A Virtuous Woman Helps the Needy
She stretches out her hand to the poor, yea she reached forth her hands to the needy. 21 She is not afraid of the snow for her household; for all her household are clothed with scarlet. 22 she maketh herself coverings of tapestry; her clothing is silk and purple. 23 her husband is known in the gates, when he sits among the elders of the land. 24 She taketh fine linen and sells it; and delivereth girdles unto the merchant. 25 Strength and honor are her clothing; and she shall rejoice in time to come.

A Virtuous Woman Speaks Wisdom

She openeth her mouth with wisdom; and in her tongue is the law of kindness. She locket well to the ways of her household, and earth not the bread of idleness. 28 Her children arise up, and call her blessed; her husband also; and he praiseth her. 29 many daughters have done virtuously but thou excellest them all. 30 Favour is deceitful, and beauty is vain; but a woman that feareth the Lord, she shall be praised. 31 Give her of the fruit of her hands; and let her own works praise her in the gates.

Becoming a Proverbs 31 woman is not about being perfect. It's about living life with purpose, diligence, forgiveness, and repentance.

A virtuous woman is stable. It's so important to be stable: having your own income, planning your future, and home ownership.

Stability is having a stable income and benefits, working a 9 to 5, or creating your own opportunity as an entrepreneur. Stability is something many people don't realize is important. When you have something, no matter how small, you can plan and build better.

At a young age, I always had an entrepreneurial spirit. I remember at age 9 or 10, my cousin and I started a manicure/pedicure business, doing people's hands and feet, but only for family members. We also ran a lemonade and Kool-Aid stand.

In middle school, I would sell candy with Kool-Aid in it. I remember going to Smart & Final, getting those sweet-sour strips and putting Kool-Aid in a zip bag. I sold it for two dollars. It was an innovative way to sell candy. I also sold other candy bars as well.

I taught myself how to braid hair. I wanted to do my hair and make money. So, I would charge people to do their hair. I was in middle school selling candy and braiding hair. I remember practicing on a Barbie doll and my hair. I would braid all my uncle's and cousin's hair, and also my Dad's. It was a source of income for me.

In high school I really worked by choice of course. I didn't get an allowance from my parents. It was me and my two sisters, so unless we really needed something, they weren't just buying things.

I went to three different high schools, Animo Charter High, Birmingham High School in California, and Nimitz High School in Texas. When I moved to Texas at age 17, I started working a real job. I worked at a snow cone place as my first job in Texas. My neighbors were the owners. After a few months there, I applied to McDonalds for a cashier's position. I worked there for a few months. I would ride my bike to work or catch a ride from friends. I didn't have a car in high school, but I didn't let that stop me, I was determined to have the things I wanted. So I upgraded to the mall and worked at Champs in Deerbrook Mall for a few months, then I worked at Airserv. I took tickets from people at the airport. It was international, and I loved seeing people from all over the world. I was a senior and working two jobs, at Champs and the airport. Talk about grinding, I would go from one job to the other and then work on the weekends. I would have to be at the airport at 5am. I wanted to buy my senior stuff; prom was coming up; graduation; photos; and a yearbook. I wanted to have all of those things that a graduating senior needs for high school.

Then, I started working at Kay Jewelers during my freshman year in college. Basically, at this time of my life I was working and had no guidance, no one telling me where I should invest my money or what to get in place for myself, business ideas or nothing.

I wasted money buying clothes, shoes and renting a big house (paying $2,400 per month) and that should have been a mortgage. I had to learn a lot on my own; I wanted a certain lifestyle and certain things, but I wasn't sure how to get them. But I was determined to figure it out. I opened my first checking account and applied for my first credit card to buy schoolbooks.

What I'm trying to say is I jumped around job to job with no plan or stability. I was working harder, not smarter. All during my 20s I was making fast money and had no constructive guidance, no plan, besides wanting to be a journalist and media proprietor. To grow in my career, I invested in myself. From broadcasting school to trips to cover events to volunteering to do things for free to build my name and experience. I even started my own platform, JTV. When you are an entrepreneur, money comes and goes, it's fast-paced. You are on a hustle everyday planning how you are going to get paid. Today at 30 years old, I'm finally getting more stable. I had to get a job where I could invest in my business and not struggle to do it. I have a salaried income now, with benefits and insurance. Financially I can plan better for my business. I just bought my first house, no more renting, because I can now show more stability and steady income. At the same time, I am able to build my own business and have a more legit plan.

Being an entrepreneur is great, however, until you get your business on its feet, get a stable income so you can build, strategize, and have a more fruitful and rewarding plan.

At age 27, someone just shared this with me, and I applied it. It made sense. I saw it clearly. Even if you don't want to be an entrepreneur, you, as a powerful woman, need to give yourself stability and ownership. Own some property. Know that you are okay, and you are prepared. Knowing that you have equity in something gives you more confidence. Owning something — a business, car, home, investments; whatever that is for you, OWN IT!

It's also important to be confident in who you are as a WOMAN. Loving yourself and the uniqueness and value you bring to anything you are a part of is important. In life you will have challenges and it will make you feel like you're not equipped or not enough. Here are some secrets to help you build your confidence back up; so you can focus on the solutions.

A Few Confident Woman Reminders

- A confident woman knows that she is loved with no doubt: Period (She doesn't fear being unloved because she knows first and foremost that God loves her unconditionally. To be whole and complete, we need to know we are loved and to love ourselves.) The love you put in yourself will be what you attract.

- A confident woman refuses to live in fear. (That doesn't mean that we will never feel fear, but it does mean that we will not allow it to rule our decisions and actions.) Continue to do it, even if you are afraid. Keep pushing forward. Light is at the end of the tunnel.

- A confident woman is positive (Being positive is a choice. And so is being negative. It solely depends on what you choose to speak, think, and act. It's the product of your repetitive behavior) Pour positivity into yourself daily. Focus on the solutions, not the problems.

- A confident woman recovers from setbacks (Each action you take is a steppingstone that gets you closer to your destiny, even if that step results in a failure. Stop allowing your mistakes to stop you and let them lead you to your destiny.) You will make mistakes that are part of life and growing. Learn from those mistakes.

- A confident woman avoids comparison (A confident woman is able to appreciate the gifts of others while still being sure that her gifts are just as remarkable, even if those gifts look different. Your uniqueness is a showcase of God's creativity. He will never help you become someone else so cherish how he's created you, so find contentment in that.) Know that you bring a different approach to anything you are a part of. You're in your own lane. You have your own table that when you're ready, you can attach it to theirs.

- A confident woman takes action (There are two types of people in the world. The ones who wait for something to happen and the ones who make something happen.) Do what you can do.

- A confident woman does not live in "if only" and "what if". (If you will give God what you have, no matter how little or ineffective you may think it is, God will use it and give you back more than you gave Him.) Leave the past in the past. What you went through, matured you, advanced you, next leveled you. Stay focused on the now and the present.

Know that you are a virtuous woman, a stable woman, and a confident woman!

Ask Yourself the Following Questions

When do you feel your best?

....

What's your plan to continue to stay or become stable?

....

What do you value?

....

What song puts you in your Boss Character Mood?

....

What do you want to own?

....

What three habits/ routine do you think you will need to do consistently to reach your goals?

....

Say it with me: "I am the prize, the trophy, the jewel. The woman that adds value and holds value." The foundation of life and creativity comes from you. Make sure when you walk, you walk into your greatness. You can't be duplicated. You are 1 of 1. Embrace the majesty of your divine geometry. The world will be transformed by your presence and in the people you encounter to converse with.

Leave a little light with everyone you meet.

Here are a few quotes from women that are good to remember...

Oprah Winfrey "Anything you can imagine you can create."

Michelle Obama - "Don't be afraid, be focused, be determined, be hopeful, be empowered."

Betty Shabazz, "I wish you Power, that equals your intelligence and your strength. I wish you success that equals your talent and determination and I wish you faith. Most people can't deal with reality but indulge heavily in fantasy AND FEAR."

Coretta Scott King, "It doesn't matter how strong your opinions are, if you don't use your power for positive change, you are indeed part of the problem."

Now the fact that you are a virtuous woman, a stable woman, and a confident woman, you hold the key to your destiny. These 3 keys have been unlocked...

POWERFUL WOMAN FACTS

Oprah Winfrey

Oprah was fired from her first television job in Baltimore, but she didn't let that deter her from dominating the talk-show field for 25 years. She ultimately became the first Black female billionaire and the world's richest African American woman.

Dolly Parton

She is more than just a head full of blonde hair with a beautiful singing voice. In 1995 Dolly Parton founded the Imagination Library, a charity devoted to championing literacy for children. Dollywood, her amusement park in Pigeon Forge, Tennessee, also provides more than 3,000 jobs.

CHAPTER 4

HER CALLING: PURPOSE NOT PERFECTION

Your calling is uniquely designed by God. The Creator has created you to perform to show up and use all of your capabilities. This life that you were given has purpose. The journey you will walk will not be perfect. There will be distractions, road bumps, detours, accidents, gas stops and repairmen along the way. If you keep moving and pushing forward through the obstacles, you will get to your destiny. You lack nothing. You were given everything you need to survive. Everything else you need on this journey will come to you as long as you stay focused on your life assignment. Your inner self will guide you and direct you. Walk into your destiny.

Each person is born with a unique purpose. Identifying, acknowledging, and honoring this purpose is perhaps the most important action successful people take. You should take the time to understand what you are here to do and then pursue that with passion and enthusiasm. For some people, their purpose and passion in life is obvious and clear. We're born with a set of talents, and through persistent practice, we develop our talents into skills.

For some people, it's not easy to identify a passion. You may have even asked yourself at one point or another, "What should I do with my life?" What is my passion?" or "What is my life purpose?

Here are some ways to help you find your life's passion and true purpose.

1. **Explore the things you love to do and what comes easy to you**. We are all born with a deep and meaningful purpose that we must discover. Your purpose is not something you need to make up; it's already there. You must uncover it in order to create the life you want. You can begin to discover your passion or your purpose by exploring two things.

   What do you love to do?

   What comes easily to you?

   What could you do every day and not get paid?

Of course, it takes work to develop your talents—even the most gifted musician still must practice, but it should feel natural, like rowing downstream rather than upstream. For me figuring out my purpose, I had an idea at age 17. We did a personality test in class. I remember when the question came about, What I wanted to do? I went down the list. I thought I wanted to be in the WNBA. I was a tomboy until my senior year in high school. I loved sports. So, I said If I want to be the best basketball player, I will have to practice every day, or I'll be playing on the road in a game. It would literally be my life. After thinking about it, I said, "No, I don't like it that much to do it every day." Then, I thought I wanted to be a lawyer. I love to debate and make my point. The sound of it was neat. I thought about how I barely follow the laws or know them, but for me to be the best, I would have to study every day and make sure I knew all the new laws, etc. I was like, "no, that doesn't flow for me either." Next, I thought about what I do naturally. I thought about how I like meeting new people and hearing about their lives and how they overcame certain challenges. I was always curious to learn about someone new. I said to myself, "hmmm an interviewer could work. Wait, that's a journalist." I thought about my personality and what would feel like I'm not working, and it flowed naturally-- a profession that I really can enjoy. Everything I do stems from me learning and sharing what I learned from certain interviews or people that I meet.

2. **Ask yourself what qualities you enjoy expressing the most to the world.** First ask yourself, what are two qualities I most enjoy expressing? Mine are love and joy. Second, ask yourself, what are two ways that I most enjoy expressing these qualities? Mine are inspiring and empowering people. Anything I am a part of is to uplift people to be their best.

3. **Create a life purpose statement.** Take a few moments and write a description of what the world would look like if it were operating perfectly according to you. For example: In my perfect world, everybody is living abundantly, fulfilling their highest vision where they are doing, being, creating, and having everything they want. Then combine all three into one statement, and you will have a clear idea of your purpose.

4. **Follow your inner GPS (What is your heart telling you?)** What if I told you that you have your own guidance system within you that can help you get from where you are in life to where you want to go? Neat, huh! It's called your inner GPS. Your inner GPS is like the GPS System you use in your car or

on your phone. A lot of times people use it for wherever they go. What about that inner GPS? It tells you how to get from point A to point B. First you have to *decide where you want to go.* Clarify your vision, then lock into your destination through goal setting, affirmations, and visualization, and then start taking the actions that will move you in the right direction. With every picture you visualize in your mind, you're "inputting" the destination you want to get to. Every time you express a preference for something, you are expressing an intention. Whether it's a table by the window, front row seats at a conference, first-class tickets, a room with an ocean view, or a loving relationship. All these images and thoughts are sending requests to the universe. If you stay out of its way, (meaning you don't interrupt the process with a stream of negative thoughts, doubts, and fears), your inner GPS will keep unfolding the next steps along your route as you continue to move forward. You will get a feeling or thought of what your next move should be. In other words, once you clarify and then stay focused on your vision (you can do this with a vision board/ lifestyle board or through meditation), the exact steps will keep appearing along the way in the form of accessing internal guidance, creating ideas, and new opportunities.

5. **Be clear about your life's purpose.** Once you are clear about what you want and keep your mind constantly focused on it, the how will keep showing up, sometimes just when you need it and not a moment earlier. You were born with an inner guidance that tells you when you are on or off course by the amount of joy you are experiencing. You will know the things that bring you the greatest joy are in alignment with your purpose and will get you to where you want to go. When

you present your goals to the universe with all its powerful technology, you will be surprised and dazzled by what it delivers. This is where the magic and miracles really happen. Take some time to think honestly and openly about where you currently are in your life and what you want to do with your life.

Think about the times you used to dream or have ideas. Don't doubt yourself, you can do anything you put your mind to. Anything is possible.

Next, think about where you would like to be. If your life were perfect right now, what would it look like? What kind of job or business would you have and where would you be living? By continually doing this, you'll send powerful triggers to your subconscious mind to help you get there. It's truly amazing. Once what you start seeing starts to happen.

6. **Align your goals with your life's purpose and passions.** We're all gifted with a set of talents and interests that tell us what we are supposed to be doing. Once you know what your life purpose is, organize all your activities around it. Everything you do should be an expression of your purpose. From the events you attend to the people you hang around. If the activity or goal doesn't fit that formula, don't work on it. Aligning with your purpose is most critical when setting professional goals. When it comes to personal goals, you have more flexibility. If you want to learn how to play the piano or do a back flip, do so. Sign up for the classes.

If your goal is to get fit and lose weight, move ahead with confidence. You know what you need to do. Start with a habit of clean eating. Then, nurturing yourself emotionally, physically, and spiritually will make you more energized, resilient, and motivated to live your purpose on the professional front. However, don't ignore the signs that your job or career is not right for you. If you dread Monday mornings and live for the weekends, it may be a sign that it's time to follow your heart and pursue the work you long to do.

7. **Lean into your true-life purpose.** Once you have gained more clarity about your purpose, you don't need to completely repair your life all at once. Instead, just lean into it, bit by bit. Start living your purpose a little more fully every day and pay attention to the feedback you are receiving from others in terms of the results you are producing, and also to how you are feeling. Remember, it's your life, you are responsible for you and your actions.

These seven tips will help you find your passion and purpose. It's about purpose, not perfection. All you can control in life is how you respond to life.

You have capabilities that you were born with. You have instinct, a voice, the ability to multitask, to teach, to grow, and build things. You are capable of so much. A woman's role continues to evolve as she gets older. Her mind blossoms and continues to create. She is then able to tap into her master mind and attract everything she wants and needs, because she understands timing and seizes the opportunity. Every time an opportunity presents itself, she's prepared. And when there isn't an opportunity, she creates one.

Love, life, and magic are inside of her. At the tip of her fingers, she can create the life she wants because God has given her the vision of the life He designed her to live. But it's up to her to make wise choices and make it her reality. She must ask questions along the way and listen to herself in every move she makes.

God has given you the power to live out your vision from the moment he created you. It's up to you to acknowledge it, see it, understand it, and create it. The road to realizing your highest good is not going to be flawless. I repeat, along the journey, as you are building your vision, remember you are living out your purpose and everything's not going to be perfect. Consistency and persistence will become perfection. Because you will be moving closer to completing the vision daily, do something towards your vision, big or small, every day. You will look up and see yourself there.

Choose passion and purpose over perfection. Passion can be developed by breaking out of your comfort zone and exploring different options. When you are passionate about something, you find it easy. You realize you're getting better than others, and fast. That rising excitement you feel is your passion, and that passion makes you come back for more, improving your skills, and compounding your strengths. Passion is in the doing. Even when you don't feel like doing something, you're pushing and continuing to do it will create the energy you need to complete it.

Here are some questions to bring clarity:

What are you passionate about?

....

What do you feel your purpose is?

....

What do you wish was perfect? (How can you make it better?)

....

What are five things you love about yourself?

....

Are you living in your purpose? (If not, how are you going to start?)

....

What are three goals you have for the week?

....

Where's your happy place or space? (Create one or pay attention to where you go that makes you happy)

Now every day isn't going to be perfect, but it still doesn't mean that today doesn't have a purpose.

Your purpose, not perfection, has been unlocked....

POWERFUL WOMAN FACTS

Madam C. J. Walker

(1867-1919) was lauded as "the first black woman millionaire in America" for her successful line of hair care products. Born Sarah Breedlove, she was widowed by age 20 and took work as a laundress. After seeking treatment for hair loss, she developed the "Walker System" and sold her homemade products directly to Black women.

Katherine Graham

When Katherine Graham, known as "KAY," took over the leadership of The Washington Company in 1972. She became the first woman to be CEO of a fortune 500 company. Under her leadership, The Washington Post flourished and famously broke the story of the Watergate scandal to the world.

Janet Guthrie

Guthrie was an aerospace engineer, training to be an aerospace engineer and astronaut, when she was cut from the space program because she didn't have her PhD. She turned to car racing instead and became the first woman to qualify for the Daytona 500 and Indianapolis 500.

CHAPTER 5

VALUES AND PRINCIPLES REQUIRE DISCIPLINE

A woman must have morals, values, and principles. Her positive body language and practicing etiquette is external evidence of the standards she possesses. Her discipline and preparation always keep her ahead in any situation. She knows her value and will not stoop to anyone else's level that does not align with or exceeds her own. Her principles show her strength, her body language and etiquette leave a positive imprint on whomever she converses with.

A lady will always be treated like a lady if she carries herself with poise and grace. Let me share with you a few things to remember about Mannerisms of a Lady:

- Always steer clear of gossip chains. It's unbecoming to spread gossip, and when you're the focus of the gossip, it's quite hurtful. Everyone's fighting their own battles.

- When you're posting on social media, ask yourself if my grandmother or children saw this photo on Facebook/Instagram/Twitter/TikTok, would they be proud of it? Is this the message I want to put out there? I'm sure you look amazing in your new polka dot bikini selfie, and last night at the club you looked stunning, but just think before you post.

- Always remember your "please" and "thank you." Simple but true, the words, "please" and "thank you" make the world a happier and more polite place.

- Beware of being someone who brags. Nobody likes a braggart. If you paid a lot for the Chanel bag, have a gorgeous summer house in Nantucket, and a yacht in St. Tropez, your closest friends will find out, eventually. There is nothing as refined and attractive as humility.

- Talk about what you have going on, when communicating at events, see how you can collaborate with others if you see fit.

- Watch your cocktails. It's tough to be elegant after one too many cocktails. Always try to have water in between drinks if you can. And if you've had too much to drink, excuse yourself and leave.

- Table manners. Read a refresher course on table manners before a formal dinner party or wedding. It can never hurt.

- Make sure you don't place your elbows on the table.

- Get a Manicure. Even if you don't wear polish, keep your hands neat. The hands are often a central focus. If you're in desperate need of a manicure, take off your polish and buff your nails.

- Chewing gum. If you're chewing gum in public, make sure not to smack it. Also, discard gum before a dinner, meeting, or an interview.

- Hemlines. When wearing a skirt or dress, make sure it fully covers your posterior-- your cheeks.

- Engage in conversation. When at the dinner table, at a wedding, or spending time with family and friends, get off your phone. Remember conversation is a true art, and at the end of the day, it's the relationships you have with people in real life that will shape your life, not the Instagram photo you just liked.
- Try to leave some imagination to your outfit.
- Be kind, gracious, and confident. This is the trinity of being a modern lady.

Knowing that you are applying these modern day tips to being a lady, you will be known as that. A lady also has values and principles. She must stand for something, or she will fall for anything. As you stand your ground regarding your values, you must be consistent. Consistency is a key to success. To achieve whatever you want, you must do something every day toward getting it, whether it's big or small. You will get closer to what you want to receive.

It can be small or big if you are working on it daily. You can become what you want to become. You can have what you want. A powerful woman is consistent because she knows what a leader is. That is a woman who gets what she wants because she is consistent.

So many times, I have started and stopped things only to pick back up where I left off. It wasn't until I reaped the rewards of being consistent that I was able to make a permanent change. That's when I started completing projects and celebrating every step of the way because I was moving forward. Everything has a process, it's up to you to determine the process.

Things I wanted started working in my favor. It came to me. I was able to see clearly what I wanted to accomplish and started the work. The famous quote, "Faith without works is dead," is true. Everything requires some form of action whether it's acquiring money, getting wisdom, losing weight, wanting to build my brand, or wanting to be a good mother, wife or cook. I had to put the time in to get better at those things. If every day you read a little something, watch something or put action towards it, I'm telling you; you will have it. You must keep feeding yourself the knowledge you need to have to become and have what you really want. Set a goal this week to learn more information about it.

If you are not building yourself daily or learning new things, you are doing the opposite. You will be getting dull, lazy, and falling apart.

Let me remind you that you are living. That's enough energy right there, so everything you are a part of, you add value and life to it.

Let's Talk About Values.

- Freedom
- Efficiency
- Respect
- Gratitude/ Appreciation
- Kindness
- Patience
- Integrity
- Spirituality
- Learning
- Vision
- Justice
- Courage
- Loyalty

- Integrity
- Responsibility
- Servant Leadership

Those were some values I have.

Here's Some descriptive Woman VALUES:

1. Holding an Evolutionary Perspective

   She strives to live in the knowledge that the creative intelligence that gave birth to the universe is not separate from her true self. She knows that all the ways that she is conditioned—biologically, socially, and psychologically — are not personal to her, but are a part and parcel of a universal developmental process.

2. Trusting in Life

   Through letting go of her need to control repeatedly, she has discovered the empty ground of being that lies at the depth of herself. This profound experience of liberation frees her at the deepest level. As a result, she is at ease, manifesting an undefended innocence, dignity, and independence of spirit.

3. Taking Responsibility for Evolution

   Knowing that the entire developmental process is one, she endeavors to take full responsibility for evolving her own consciousness, realizing that her development moves the leading edge forward for all womankind.

4. Realizing Unity with Other Women

   She relaxes more and more into a unity with other women as she refuses to act out of the nearly universal compulsion for women to separate from and compete with each other. She doesn't deny that this compulsion, which has been key to women's survival in the past, operates in her psyche, nor is she afraid or ashamed of it, but she works to keep her focus on evolving her relationship with women through trust, transparency, and a passion to create the future.

5. Being Emotionally Rational

   Despite how overwhelming any emotional experience may be, she strives for objectivity and aspires to liberate her power of choice so that she is no longer trapped by fears and desires rooted in her biological and cultural conditioning. She is developing the emotional maturity to not dis-integrate and give in to ancient survival impulses when she finds herself under pressure.

6. Standing Autonomously and Not Wavering

   Rather than gauging her responses by what she thinks others want and need, she is cultivating a radical autonomy, grounded in her longing for liberation and her passion for the evolution of consciousness. She increasingly finds manipulative game-playing distasteful, and craves being simple, straight, and clear in her relationships with others.

7. Relinquishing Sexual Power

   She is awake to how deeply identified she is with her sexual power and how instinctive it is to use it to get what she wants. Aspiring to drop this fundamental identification, she finds that sexual relationships become more straightforward and less of a priority and marker of personal success. The more she succeeds in this aspiration, the more she discovers a profound intimacy with others that is not related to sexuality at all.

8. Leading by Example:

    Dropping the many masks of pretense and self-image, she strives for a rare vulnerability and authenticity that is not emotional but comes from being unafraid of the impulses and motivations that drive women. She is discovering a deep confidence that is not edged with hardness but founded in transparency and humility. She is willing to step forward and be a pioneer and does not abuse the power that comes with leadership.

9. Being Trustworthy

    Resisting the temptation to be dishonest or inauthentic under scrutiny, she desires to act with integrity so that her word is her bond. She aspires to be consistently true to a higher purpose, no matter what personal challenges she faces.

10. Emotionally Stable

    Relatively secure of herself and of her own worth, not going to make public drama, not excessively anxious, no wild mood swings, generally positive and uplifting. Emotionally stable doesn't mean she doesn't cry or that she never gets angry. It doesn't mean she can't have a nervous breakdown or have bouts of slight depression and self-doubt. Those are normal parts of life and dealing with them openly is actually another sign of high value.

11. Knows When to Set Boundaries

    The high value woman is pleasant and welcoming, but she's not pushover and knows when it's time to take a stand and defend her boundaries. If you're not holding your end of the relationship, she'll let you know that. When a boss is disrespectful to her, she knows how to demand the respect she deserves. Her rule of life is that she is not disrespectful to anyone, and people have no right to be disrespectful to her.

12. Have a Growth Mindset & Don't Take Things Personally

Women with a growth mindset are resilient to criticism, look for ways to improve, enjoy challenges, approach problems with a "we can do it" attitude.

13. Socially Skilled

Great social skills are important for women. In a way indeed, we can say that the ability to effortlessly form friendships is a sign of femininity. Some basic social skills are conversation, making friends, small talk, getting to know people, bonding.

14. Family

Family is important because it provides love, support, and a framework of values to each of its members. Family members teach each other, serve one another, and share life's joys and sorrows. Families Provide a setting for personal growth. Family is the first important influence in a child's life.

15. Forgiveness

Forgiveness is when you stop feeling angry or resentful toward someone for an offense, flaw, or mistake. It helps you move forward with your life. It begins your healing process. It removes the anger and malice from your heart. You're no longer giving someone else authority over your mind and heart.

16. Helping Others

Volunteering your time, money, or energy to help others doesn't just make the world better, it also makes you better.

Giving back to the community boosts your happiness, health, and a sense of wellbeing.

What does the word "values" mean to you personally?

....

What are some values you live by?

....

What change would you like to see in the world?

....

Do your values show up in your actions or your decision making?

....

Let's talk about PRINCIPLES.

Principle- A fundamental truth or proposition that serves as the foundation for a system of belief or behavior or for a chain of reasoning.

Here are some principles to guide you:

- Love more. Not just people or things, but yourself.
- Be vigilant with your thoughts. Be mindful of your thoughts and don't let them consume you.
- Forgive frequently.
- Realize that your ability to care for someone is one of the greatest assets.
- Remember that you are greater than your problems

- Use your struggles to grow stronger.
- Learn to be comfortable in your own skin.
- Know that anything is possible.
- Make a difference to one, the many will follow.
- Planning is important.
- Prioritize your goals and objectives.
- Listen carefully and compassionately.
- Integrity is key to everything you do.
- Never stop learning.
- Practice mindfulness.
- Pursue regular personal development.
- Attitude is everything.
- Be of service to others.
- Character is more important you're your reputation.
- Let go of worry, fear, and anxiety.
- Pursue excellence.
- Share your knowledge.
- See unexpected inconveniences as adventures.
- Choose peace and happiness. (It's your choice)

These are some principles I live by.

What are your top principles?

....

Do your actions and decisions stem from your principles?

....

Now that we have talked about values and principles, let's talk about discipline and how to gain it.

Discipline is an art that should be mastered

Studies show that people with self-discipline are happier. People with a higher degree of self-control spend less time debating whether to indulge in behaviors that are detrimental to their health and are able to make positive decisions more easily. They don't let impulses or feelings dictate their choices. Instead, they make levelheaded decisions. As a result, they tend to feel more satisfied with their lives.

Some ways to Gain Self Discipline

1. Remove all temptations

    You know the old saying, "out of sight, out of mind." The first step is removing all temptations and distractions from your environment is crucial when working to improve your self-discipline.}

2. Eat often and healthy

    Studies have shown that low blood sugar often weakens a person's resolve. When you're hungry, your ability to concentrate suffers as your brain is not functioning to its highest potential. You are much more likely to have a weakened sense of self-control in all areas of your life-diet, exercise, work, relationships; you name it. In order to stay on track, it's important that you stayed fueled throughout the day with healthy snacks and meals every few hours.

3. Don't wait for it to "feel right"

   Improving your self-discipline means changing up your normal routine, which can be uncomfortable and awkward at first. Whatever you need to do, just do it.

4. Schedule breaks, treats, and rewards for yourself.

   Having self-discipline does not mean your new regimen need to be entirely cold turkey, or hardcore, giving yourself zero wiggle room often results in failures, disappointments and giving into your old ways. While practicing self-control, schedule specific breaks, treats, and rewards for yourself. Set aside a day out of the week to treat yourself.

5. Forgive yourself and move forward.

   The key is to keep moving forward, when you have a setback, acknowledge what caused it and move on. It is easy to get wrapped up in guilt, anger, or frustration, but these emotions will not help build or improve self-discipline. Instead, use the hiccups in your plan as learning experiences for the future. Forgive yourself and get back in the saddle ASAP. Forgive yourself and keep pushing forward.

   In order to change something, you are doing (bad habit), you will have to replace it with something else. Just stopping will cause you being back to doing the same thing. But when you replace it, you can make the change forever.

   Discipline is the source of a champion. You must have discipline to be great. Your principles and values revolve around you having discipline, because there are things you will do and won't do. You have character; you have morals.

   You can do it!

What is one thing you're going to tell yourself to stay disciplined?

....

Do you have a bad habit? If so, what are you going to replace it with?

....

What was one of the ways from above that you're going to use to gain discipline?

....

You have unlocked your principles and values; remember you have the discipline you need.

Fun Fact:

Three things that are important to me
in any relationship:
Trust, Communication, and Respect.
Those are must haves for any relationship to work.

POWER WOMAN FACTS

Serena Williams

Serena Williams is one of the greatest female tennis stars of all time. Serena Williams is known for her powerful serves and aggressive playing style. Her achievements on and off the court show her strength and perseverance. Serena Williams was born on September 26, 1981, in Saginaw, Michigan.

Misty Copeland

Misty Copeland made history in 2015 when she became the first African American female Principal Dancer with the American Ballet

Theatre in the organization's 75 years. She's faced racism and criticism for her strong legs and core in a field where convention favors dancers with extremely thin limbs and fair skin. Copeland's innate talent as a dancer has brought her much success; in 2015 she was named Glamour's "Woman of The Year" as well as one of ESPN's "Impact 25" athletes who have had the greatest impact for women in sports.

Katherine Switzer

In 1967, Kathrine Switzer entered the Boston Marathon five years before women were officially allowed to run the race. During the race, Switzer was chased by a man trying to tear her race number bib off. She finished the race in four hours and 20 minutes, becoming the first woman in America to run in an official marathon race.

CHAPTER 6

INTUITION
(PHYSICAL VS SPIRITUAL)

Intuition is the ability to understand something immediately, without the need for conscious reasoning. We are all spirit beings that live in the human body — Humus- dirt body. We are spirit beings, so our senses are intact. Have you ever had a feeling about something and later on it happened?

For example: Let's say you have a thought about grabbing an object at home. Something told you to grab an umbrella or a snack; But you didn't. You said I'll be fine; it's not raining now, and I'm not hungry. Then, as soon as you get in the car and start driving, it starts pouring down rain and your stomach growls. You then say, "I should've listened to myself and just grabbed those things."

That's your intuition talking to your inner voice. Guiding you. Your knowledge/ wisdom voice speaking to you. Your inner voice guides you and gives insight into the future or your next move — how you should move and what you should do. It's very important to listen to yourself. It's also important that you show yourself gratitude for what you are accomplishing.

It is common to think of intuition as a magical phenomenon, but hunches are actually formed on the basis of past experience and cumulative knowledge.

To Align Your Personality With Your Soul

You must train your intuition; you must trust the small voice inside of you which tells you exactly what to say and what to decide.

Practice listening to your intuition, your inner voice; ask questions, be curious, see what you see, hear what you hear. Then act upon what you know to be true. These intuitive powers were given to your soul at birth.

What is intuition? It is a natural power that we possess. It is that inner voice inside of us that speaks to us even when we don't have any physical proof. It can be hard for many people to believe in the power of our intuition because some people can't believe in something that they can't see. Some people only believe in what is tangible.

A woman's intuition is extremely powerful and can help us when we are making decisions.

Our intuition can help us choose the right path when we are presented with a difficult issue. A woman's intuition is almost like magic. We are able to give ourselves the answers that we have searched for without having to hear them from another. All we have to do is in tune with ourselves and allow ourselves to feel. Intuition is a power inside of us that we need to pay attention to, cultivate, and strengthen.

There are so many answers that live within us. We are so powerful. Women are powerful. Our intuition is powerful. Follow it.

Here Are Three Ways to Strengthen Your Intuition

1. Self-Reflect

    Take the time to know yourself internally. This is extremely
    important. You have to dig really deep and get to know the
    deepest parts of your being so that you can understand how
    you function. It will be easier to decipher what sits well with
    you and what doesn't when you go through this process.
    Your intuition will be strengthened because you will know
    what is for you and what isn't. The decision-making process
    will be easier.

2. Listen to Your Inner Voice

    There will be a voice inside of you that will allow you to know
    when something feels wrong. You can just feel it. Do not
    silence that voice. Listen to it and then weigh the positives
    and the negatives. It will not always be right, but it usually is.

3. Practice Following Your Intuition More and More Each Day

    Listen, do not neglect what doesn't sit well with your heart
    and with your spirit. Don't neglect how something makes
    you feel. Take the time to reflect on how things make you feel
    in the moment and ask yourself why I am feeling this way
    then act accordingly. Trust your gut.

When we have a big question or an important decision to
make, many of us look outside of ourselves for the answers. We
turn to Google. We get advice from our friends and family. We read
books or consult the teachings of experts. Yet we often neglect to
consult the most important authority of all: our own intuition.

Your subconscious mind is the source of your hidden genius
and will always provide you with the knowledge you need to move

forward in the right direction. This is true for all people, not just those who consider themselves to be psychic or highly intuitive.

Consider this: Have you ever been thinking about someone–and out of the blue the phone rings and that exact person is on the line?

Or have you ever felt like someone is watching you–and when you turn around you see someone staring at you from some distance away?

These are just two common examples of your intuition at work. Just like memory, critical thinking, and intellect, your intuition is a mental muscle you can strengthen and used to create success and become the best possible version of yourself.

Here are some ways on how to develop your intuition and leverage it to make wiser, more soul-inspired decisions for your life.

1. Recognize when your intuition speaks

   First of all, in order to be able to use your intuition, you must be able to recognize it when it speaks to you. Intuition usually isn't loud or demanding–it's subtle and communicates in different ways for different people.

   For example, you may receive visual messages, such as images that appear in quick flashes or visions that unfold slowly, like a movie.

   Your intuition might speak to you as a hunch, a thought, or in words. You may even be able to enter into a dialogue with your intuition to get more information and clarity.

   Alternatively, your intuition may speak to you in physical sensations, such as goose bumps, discomfort in your gut, a feeling of relief, or a sour taste in your mouth.

You may receive intuitive messages through your emotions, such as feelings of uneasiness or confusion when your inner wisdom is steering you away from something–or feelings of euphoria and profound peace when you're being guided down a path that will lead you to greater personal joy and abundance.

Sometimes intuition messages are simply a deep sense of knowing and certainty. If you've ever felt that you knew something to be true in the depths of your heart or soul, chances are it was a message from your intuition.

2. Deepen your intuition through meditation

   Focus in order to access your intuition, you need to deepen your connection to it–and meditation is an excellent tool for this. Regular meditation will help you clear your mind of distractions and teach you how to better recognize the subtle impulses from within.

   I recommend you set aside time each day to meditate on your own, or use guided meditations.

   It doesn't have to be long–even 10 minutes a day will yield powerful results and will make it much easier for you to notice your intuition when it speaks to you through words, images, emotions, or physical sensations.

3. Dedicate time to listen to your intuition each day

   Life is busy, and in the rush to cross off items on our daily to-do lists, it is easy to forget to stop and tune into our higher intelligence. But your most valuable wisdom comes when you are most open to receiving it.

That's why I encourage you to devote time every day–multiple times a day, if necessary–to consciously give your intuition the center stage. This is especially important when you're being asked to make any important decisions. Be sure to take some time to sit with your intuition and look inside yourself for the answers before you choose which path to take.

4. Ask questions

Receiving wisdom from your intuition shouldn't be a passive experience. Get specific about the information you need and what kind of answers you're looking for. The more clearly you present your questions to your innate wisdom, the clearer the answers will be for you.

5. Write down your answers

Either record yourself speaking or write it down in your notes on your phone. Intuitive messages are subtle and can fade from your conscious mind very quickly unless you take action to record them. If your intuitive insights are not captured within 37 seconds, they will probably never be recalled again.

Journal writing is a highly effective way to access your intuition and capture its wisdom. I suggest you make a regular practice of journaling for just five or ten minutes a day–you'll be amazed at the clarity of what comes through!

6. Take immediate action

The Universe rewards those who take action–and so does your intuition. When you act on the information you receive from your inner source of wisdom, you open the channel between your subconscious and conscious mind even wider and will receive more intuitive messages that are stronger and easier for you to hear and act on. Pay attention.

7. Trust yourself

    The more faith you demonstrate in your intuition, the greater the results will be.

    Whether you want to make better decisions, solve problems faster, or create winning plans for your life, you will achieve your goals faster and more effectively when you tune into your intuition and listen to what your inner wisdom says.

Do you listen to your intuition?

....

Will you start trusting yourself more when it comes to decisions?

....

Trust that your intuition has been unlocked.

POWER WOMAN FACTS

Maya Angelou

Memoirist, poet, civil rights activist Maya Angelou broke boundaries by becoming one of the first African American women to write openly and publicly about her private life. Since publishing I Know Why the Caged Bird Sings in 1969, she has forged extra space for Black feminist writing, and has even influenced hip-hop artists like Nicki Minaj and Tupac Shakur.

Angela Merkel

In 2005, Angela Merkel was elected as Chancellor of Germany, making her the first woman to ever hold that position. She was chosen as "Person of The Year," in 2015 by *Time* magazine, who called her "the most powerful woman in the world."

Judy Hehr

Judy is a child of God, wife to Bob and Mother. She retired from her ten-year sales career in the printing industry to embrace more fully, her vocation as wife and mother. Today she devotes her talent for speaking, coaching, and leadership development as an entrepreneur.

CHAPTER 7

LEGACY BUILDER

A legacy builder is a leader. She has stability, insurance, land, and income. She listens, teaches, and speaks wisely. She is a mother figure who positions herself to leave generational wealth to her children/family. She brings them up to live on a legacy she has created and built. A legacy where they can be further along in their journey. Where they have a head start in life.

It's important to own land; to have an insurance policy (life insurance) on yourself; and to teach by example is so important. People learn from seeing others doing it on their own. To groom the next generation, a knowledgeable woman who knows what's going on in her community and the world knows how to plan and execute her vision in a timely manner. Her family is ready to learn and is looking at her. Let's build a legacy.

Today, during an interview, I spoke with a lady about what keeps her motivated and she said "3D" -- which means three generations deep. She was telling me that's what her family believes in-- building something that can benefit three generations-- from traditions, finances, equity, principles and more. I thought to myself, "that's neat." Here I am thinking for two generations, but three! That is motivation.

I shared that because life is about living while you are here. It's about creating and building the vision that God has given you. We have the choice whether or not to bring it to life or place the vision to the side. A legacy builder can be different things to many people, I would like to share with you some forms of building a legacy.

Build a legacy by eliminating behaviors and attitudes that dilute impact. It's not enough to add positive behaviors and eliminate bad.

The only time to build legacy is now.

The only way to change legacy is to change now.

1. Dare to be joyful. Serve in ways that bring you joy. Angry, unhappy people leave sad legacies.

2. Monitor your impact on others. What are you doing when you make the biggest difference. Do more of that.

3. Develop and maximize your talent, strengths, and skills. Know yourself – Bring yourself.

4. Do what matters now. Everyone who's at the end of life says it goes by fast.

5. Seize small opportunities. Big may follow. Stop waiting to make a difference.

6. Start with those closest to you and the ones you spend the most time with.

7. Bring your best self to work and family. Everyone has at least two selves. Bring out the best one.

8. Think service not success.

9. Relax. Don't run around building a legacy. Run around making a difference.

10. Mentor. Teach at least one person a life lesson that you've learned.

The foundation of building a legacy is a deep sense of knowing-- not just what is important to you-- but what is non-negotiable. In a sense, it doesn't matter what those non-negotiables are. They could revolve around corporate culture, team building, production quality, customer service, innovation, or any one of a thousand other things. What matters is that you know what they are.

It helps to put your non-negotiables down on paper. Write a manifesto. Print off a pdf and distribute it. Revise it regularly, over time, amending the wording to clarify and hone your non-negotiables. Strip away everything that's merely a 'nice to have', until the manifesto clearly sings your legacy a cappella, uncluttered by distracting background melodies.

Decide what kind of legacy you want to create.

In order to create a powerful legacy with your life, you need to decide what contribution you want to make to the world. I suggest spending some time journaling and reflecting on the following questions:

1. If you knew with certainty that you only had five more years to live, how would you spend those years, and why?

....

2. What message do you want to send with your life to the world and to those who matter most to you?

....

3. Imagine that you are attending your own funeral. What would you want your family and friends to say about you and how you lived your life?

....

4. What do you want to be remembered for?

....

5. What do you want to pass on?

....

Sometimes we have to picture what the end looks like so that we can better position ourselves to live. Start creating your legacy today.

We all have a limited time on this planet. And yet, we often live our lives as if our time were unlimited, putting things off, thinking that we'll always have more time.

Yet the truth is that none of us knows how long we'll live. If you want to create a powerful legacy with your life, then you need to stop wasting time and start creating it today.

Look over your answers to the questions above. Based on your answers to those questions, identify three to five specific goals you can set for creating the legacy that you want. Then, for each goal, figure out the first step you can take and start taking it today!

Simplify your life and focus on the essentials. Figure out the two to four things that are most important to you and put the bulk of your energy into those activities while letting go of the rest. An Example: Building powerful connections with others, creating beautiful art, and cultivating your own spiritual growth.

Here are a few ways to leave a financial legacy to your heirs:

- Vacation Homes Make a Great Inheritance. ...
- Be Clear About Your Family Home and Personal Belongings. ...
- Create a Beneficiary IRA. ...
- Name a Child as Beneficiary for an Annuity. ...
- Use Excess Distributions for a Second-to-Death Life Insurance Policy. ...
- Gift Depreciating Stock to Charities.
- Trust Fund
- Legacy investment
- Business Account
- Factory
- Buy Land

What does your family value?

....

What are your goals for the year as a family in regard to building a legacy?

....

What do you think about building your legacy?

....

What legacy do you want to leave?

....

The question isn't whether or not you are creating a legacy. The question is whether or not you are actively creating the legacy you want to leave. Incorporate some of the suggestions above. Begin leading your life deliberately, and I have no doubt that you'll create a powerful legacy that will last for generations.

You have unlocked the key to being a legacy builder.

POWER WOMAN FACTS

Catherine
(The Czarina of Russia)

Catherine The Great ruled Russia for 34 years and is the longest-serving female leader of that country. She married Peter III.

She is still renowned in Russia as a charismatic leader, scholar, and a collector of fine art. She is also known for constructing the Winter Palace. (also known as the Hermitage), which up until recently was the largest art museum in the world.

Hedy Lamarr

Known for being a silver screen siren, Hedy Lamarr has recently been embraced as a female innovator for inventing an encrypted wireless communication system with composer George Antheil. They jointly applied for a patent in 1942, but their technology has made modern day technology like Wi-Fi, GPS, and cell phones possible.

CHAPTER 8

APPEARANCE WITH CLASS (INNER & OUTER BEAUTY)

S tanding tall can make everything else about you look and feel more attractive. The beauty of a woman is not in a facial mole. True beauty in a woman is reflected in her soul. It is the caring that she lovingly gives, the passion that she shows.

Your strength is your personality. It is who you are. That's your magnet. Build on your strength, improve on your weakness by presenting your strength. Let your life and your personality present itself first.

Embrace it, observe it, let it inspire you. Your personality is so welcoming; it's more overwhelming than any weakness. That's a powerful strength. Your appearance glows from the inside to the outside. Let your light shine so brilliantly within that you effortlessly share it with those around you.

Tap into your outer beauty:

1. Show confidence inside and out
2. Focus on what you do have, not on what you don't

3. A smile works wonders (SMILE)
4. Reinvent your look from time to time
5. Connect to others in a sensual way
6. Leave competition out of beauty
7. Replace anti-aging with healthy aging
8. See yourself as an example for the next generation
9. Walk it like you talk it
10. Be unique with your style
11. Own your look, embrace who you are

Outer beauty refers to the good quality of physical appearance while inner beauty refers to the personal traits or talents which are not straightforward to observe from the appearance. Inner beauty is far more important than outer beauty. Inner beauty simply refers to the personality of a person, including their mind and character. Outer beauty means the look, which can always be enhanced by makeup, surgery, extensions, and clothes.

"Outer beauty pleases the eye. Inner beauty captivates the Heart."- **Mandy Hale**

Enhance Your Inner Beauty

Establish a Morning Routine that creates Motivation and Inspiration. (music, scriptures, positive words)

Use food as literal "fuel" to nourish your body (protein, fruit, healthy breakfast)

Practice Mindfulness and gratitude throughout the day

Aim to give back in some way

Develop an evening routine that assists with relaxation and growth.

Show love to yourself (congratulate yourself, kiss your hand)

Qualities that Enhance Your Inner Beauty....

- Kindness. Let's put on kindness first.
- Gentleness/ Femininity. This is a tough one because sometimes gentleness can be confused with weakness.
- Modesty
- Purity
- Generosity
- Humility
- Honesty/ Commitment

Inner beauty helps you appreciate outer beauty. If you love, appreciate, and feel good about yourself, you will feel more confident about facing and interacting with other beautiful people in the world. Remember, outer beauty can give you a glance, its inner beauty that makes someone stay.

What are your flaws? Write them down. Then I want you to love them. That's part of what makes you unique.

What makes you feel beautiful?

....

Do you try new looks from time to time? (Have you ever thought of a certain look you wanted to try? Try it?)

....

Inner beauty starts with self-love and self-care, what did you do today to take care of yourself?

....

Mirror Exercise

Have a conversation with yourself in the mirror, say to yourself as you smile:

- I love the person that I am (say your full name)
- I am so proud of you, you are so smart
- You are beautiful, you got it going on
- I love the way you look with no makeup on
- Touch your face as you say this: "I love my face, my eyes, my smile, my hair, my lips and the way you blush."
- You're so creative and wise
- You complete everything you start
- Everything you dreamed of will be your reality
- Anything you want, you can have
- You are powerful, you are capable, you are enough
- You have everything you need
- You're like a magnet whatever you need comes to you
- You make wise choices
- You are loved, wanted, needed, and blessed.
- You will make a difference
- I am patient and a remarkable woman
- You only think positive thoughts and solutions
- You are successful and a multi-millionaire

You can use these and add some of your own. Make sure you are loving yourself and speaking positively to yourself. You set the tone for what and who you will attract.

"Put your good girdle on. You are going somewhere." This is a quote my great- grandmother, Byrd Ella English, would say. That's how you knew it was time to show up and be presentable.

It's time to be bold, be brave, be you.

Keep changing, keep growing, keep evolving, Keep succeeding, keep moving, keep learning from your mistakes, keep shining, through it all.

You were born to SHINE!

Your Inner Beauty and Outer Beauty are unlocked...

POWER WOMAN FACTS

Audrey Hepburn

Audrey Hepburn (born Audrey Kathleen Ruston; 4 May 1929 – 20 January 1993) was a British actress and humanitarian. Recognized as a film and fashion icon, she was ranked by the American Film Institute as the third-greatest female screen legend in Golden Age

Hollywood, and was inducted into the International Best Dressed List Hall of Fame.

Grace Kelly

Grace Kelly rose to fame as a leading Hollywood actress following her prominent role in High Noon. Along with her Academy Award-winning performance in The Country Girl, she starred in the Alfred Hitchcock films Rear Window, Dial M for Murder, and To Catch a

Thief. Kelly left Hollywood behind after marrying Prince Rainier III of Monaco in 1956, thereby becoming known as Princess Grace.

Jennifer Lynn Lopez

Jennifer Lopez was born July 24, 1969), also known by her nickname J. Lo, is an American actress, singer, dancer, fashion designer, producer, and businesswoman. In 1991, Lopez began appearing as a Fly Girl dancer on In Living Color, where she remained a regular until she decided to pursue an acting career in 1993. For her first leading role in the 1997 Selena biopic of the same name, Lopez became the first Latin actress to earn over $1 million USD for a film. She went on to star in Anaconda (1997) and Out of Sight (1998), and later establishing herself as the highest-paid Latin actress in Hollywood.

CHAPTER 9

GODDESS ENERGY

G oddess Energy is an aura of a woman being in her full femininity. Goddess energy encompasses so many elements but in its simplest form, it's a level of awareness linked to the divine spirit, it's devoid of ego, judgement or harm and deeply tied to nature, mysticism, wisdom, intuition, purity and matters of the heart.

When we are born, we are born whole and complete. Be clear on what leads you forward and what holds you back. Choose the path that leads to wisdom.

1. Release what doesn't serve you. Look in the mirror, talk to yourself and discover what is holding you back and admit it. Confirm that you want to change it, then release it to become free of it. Identify the emotions that you need to release in order to come to your true Goddess Energy. You are now free to tap into your creative side.

2. Practice stillness and quiet solitude

3. Observe, do not judge

4. Be mindful where you are putting your energy

5. Connect with divine love

Vibration is a natural high (things around us in the world causes our energy to come down.)

As you are right now, you are valuable. You don't have to do anything; just allow yourself to be.

Your Goddess Energy is calm, observe it and let it be, do not judge. Don't let events, people or things affect your inner peace. We are creators, we create our reality.

So, when something happens, ask yourself why is this certain situation triggering me? Step back and ask yourself.

Your Goddess Energy has a set amount of natural energy every day. Your physical being is spiritual energy. Be mindful, wherever your focus goes that's where your energy and power go. Ask before getting into certain conversations: "is this worth me giving my sacred, limited energy."

Listen to your intuition. Spending time in nature, doing what you love, and meditating can recharge you and give you more energy.

News, phone, and social media are things used to take away your energy. So be mindful about what you are giving your energy to.

AS A WOMAN IN HER POWER, YOU DON'T
HAVE TO GIVE YOUR POWER TO BE
ATTRACTIVE. BE IN YOUR GODDESS
ENERGY.

Embody the Goddess Energy Every day.

1. Practice self-love
2. Engage in positive thinking
3. Speak kindly of and to yourself
4. Explore, learn, and be open to new things.
5. Meditate on what you want
6. Release fear, don't worry and doubt
7. Play and creatively daydream
8. Expand your spiritual awareness
9. Open to the abundant good in life.
10. Write poetry or keep a journal
11. Watch for signs to guide your way
12. Pray or ask for what you desire
13. Keep an attitude of thankfulness

A woman that is in her power doesn't have to give up her power to be attractive. Tapping into her power is simply just being-- whether it's magnetic, sexy, smart, intelligent, in a relationship, or such. Being sexy or seductive does not mean you have to be a bimbo or doormat. The women who are smart/ educated and have substance don't want to be only in their sexual energy, as neither of these energy levels alone make her complete.

A Goddess has all things. She's sexy, seductive, magnetic, attractive and she has a beautiful, vibrant aura. She's hypnotizing. She's also smart, articulate, wise and knowledgeable of her total self. Men go crazy over a Goddess. Absolutely, men are attracted to a goddess.

You don't have to choose one side. You don't shun your sexuality. It's a huge part of your power. No, it's not used as a tool to get your way or to manipulate others. You don't intentionally provoke others in a sexual manner or tempt them for personal gain. Seduction is a part of being a woman and is a valuable tool when two consenting adults are in a casual or serious relationship. It's not being slutty. You can be sensuous and fully clothed with jewelry; be vibrant without dressing in a half-naked manner. This means you don't ever have to degrade yourself to get attention from men or anyone. Your power doesn't reside in any of those things. Attraction and being radiant has to do with your aura and goddess energy. How do you get that energy up? By self-love.

When you really love yourself from within, you're going to start vibrating at a high level. Once you are vibrating at that high level, you are going to start having the goddess energy aura. You'll feel the flow of the energy you bring, it's like a confidence high, and when it turns on, it's turned up. Trust me, you do need to be careful, because you are going to attract all kinds of things to you; and yes, it does attract a lot of unwanted attention.

Your Goddess Energy attracts them to the look, but your aura and glowing allure as a goddess is what's going to pull them in, inadvertently.

When you are glowing in your energy, not only will men be attracted to you but women, kids-- everybody. You're not going to be able to fight it off. So, you might as well accept it. Attention will be coming whether you want it or not.

It starts from loving yourself within and getting that glow and aura about you. It is then, ladies, that you can have it your way, because everybody loves you when you are in your Goddess Energy.

When people come to talk to you, you look radiant, beautiful, glowing and alluring on the outside. When you speak, your Goddess Energy shines, and they start receiving knowledge from you! At that moment, they are receiving good words and vibrations from you—Powerful, uplifting words from you.

These people are going to go away uplifted, on a higher frequency. They will go away on cloud nine after being in your presence, and they're going to keep coming back for more-- because they are not going to be able to get enough of your energy. It's so uplifting and powerful to them that they get motivated-- Spiritually, mentally, and physically-- from being around you.

You are a beautiful presentation. You are like a beautiful rose-- a product of nature. You are a beautiful and alluring flower that's pleasing to look at and emits a beautiful scent. People just love to be in your presence. That's part of being a woman.

Don't deny your beauty. Your attractiveness is part of who you are and a part of your Goddess Energy. Stand in that. Your knowledge & spiritual nature should have an equal balance, so that people don't take advantage of your balance. Stand in your spiritual balance.

Show gratitude and thankfulness, by showing love to everything around you.

Women that carry this energy stand out. They are very magnetic, very mysterious, and they also have a striking personality. Women who get what they want and have everything cause people to look at them with envy.

A Real Walking Living/Breathing Goddess.

How you can recognize a goddess operating in her energy:

- She will have a very strong presence. When she steps in the room she can be quiet as a mouse, but the people will feel her presence. When she walks in the room no matter if she tries to hide it, she will still have a strong presence

- She Has a lot of light! Because of Her energy, people will start feeling better after being in her presence. For example, they will say "wow, something about her" or "she made me feel good. Their energy is positive."

- She can light up a room. They are very, very different, not like other women... there is something peculiar about them.

- Very mysterious, they spark a lot of intrigue. People want to know a lot about them.

- They are very positive in their outlook on life, they build people up, make them feel good about a situation or life challenge.

- A Goddess is always laughing/ joking with a carefree attitude. Her spirit and soul are beautiful

- They are very intimidating to some because they are very powerful. Even though they seem like the nicest, sweetest person. People still sense a very strong powerful energy within them. You know not to mess with them.

A lot of people try to dim their light because they shine so bright, they shine without even trying. A very powerful, magical, energetic presence is prevalent.

She's very magnetic. She is herself. She is different.

Goddess Energy is the representation of the feminine energy, creativity, arts, and imagination. The Energy is inside of you. Now you know what to spark in yourself-- you already have the light and energy; you just need to turn it on.

Can you recall a time when you were walking in your goddess energy, but didn't know what it really was?

If you have never walked in your Goddess Energy, what will you do to activate it on a daily basis?

....

How can you see yourself benefiting from being more alert and aware of the Goddess Energy inside of you?

....

Inhale and exhale! Demand good energy when walking. Say to yourself, "let's go Goddess Energy..."

You have unlocked your Goddess Energy...

POWER WOMAN FACTS

Hatshepsut

Hatshepsut ruled ancient Egypt for over 20 years and was one of Egypt's most successful female pharaohs. During her reign, she was more interested in economic development and the restoration of monuments than in conquering new lands, and as a result Egypt prospered. After her death, a male heir attempted to erase Hatshepsut's name from many monuments, but in recent years she has been rediscovered and embraced as an ancient feminist hero.

Beyonce Knowles

Does Beyonce even need an introduction? Multidisciplinary artist, entrepreneur, philanthropist, fashion designer, and feminist icon.

Beyonce Knowles is a multi-platinum recording artist and the first woman to ever win six Grammys in a single night.

Cleopatra

Cleopatra VII, often referred to as simply "Cleopatra," was the last of a series of rulers called the Ptolemies who ruled Egypt for nearly 300 years. She was also the last true pharaoh of Egypt. Cleopatra ruled an empire that included Egypt, Cyprus, part of modern- day Libya and other territories in the Middle East.

CHAPTER 10

ACTIVATE POWER NOW!

When you know yourself, you are empowered. When you accept yourself, you are invincible." You are anointed. You are equipped. You are empowered. This is your season to reach new heights. May your hidden treasure within be released. New opportunities will be granted. That will draw out your power.

Be Empowered! Empowered Women Empower.

Whatever you want, go all in, and dominate it, learn it, eat it, sleep it, breathe it, and believe it.

Repeat Every Morning:

- I am the best
- I will do it
- I will take action
- I will test my limits
- Today I will dominate
- I will complete what I start

If a woman holds the power to create life, she also holds the power to create the life she wants. Sooo... (where's your pen) Start creating right now!

You are valuable! You are powerful! You are a part of the universe! A masterpiece! (Read that again!)

Remember you are the catch; you are the prize, the Queen of your throne. In business and relationships, people never forget your worth... you set your worth. True value and true beauty come from within.

Become truer to you at your core. You are beautiful, intelligent, and confident.

Setting your own path to your destiny is being completely in tune with your full self. Now it's time to tap into your conscious higher self.

Step into your higher self that God wants you to be and created you to be. You were created to create. Know that you are enough. Anything is Possible. Everything is Possible.

At your core you are flawless.

You might ask, "how do I become more in tuned with myself and know who I am?"

Do some soul searching, live life on your terms, get out of your comfort zone. Face your fears. That's how you truly know who you really are. We create a lot of who we are. From what's around us. Be the woman who can adapt to any atmosphere and evolve in different ways. Be uniquely you in every way. You are worthy just as you are right now. Show up and be a goddess and stand up for what you want. The true treasure is in your uniqueness.

1. Own what makes you different.
2. Use your talents, amplify yourself, your life just needs to make sense to you.
3. Don't let society control your power.

You are enough; you are running your own race. When God created you, he called you a masterpiece. There is Royal blood flowing in you. You have everything you need; you are powerful and anointed. Be you. What's designed for you is for you. Recognize you are enough-- talented, gifted, and one of a kind.

- When you know you are enough by yourself you get your approval from God.
- Step into who you were created to be
- You have everything you need: family, personality, beauty, and all your gifts.
- Abundance is about to follow along with the fullness of your destiny.

Say These Out Loud:
- Favor surrounds me
- Mercy and grace follow me
- I will always have what I need within my reach
- What I need comes to me
- Blessings is in my obedience
- I will do what God is asking me to do
- I already have what I need
- There are miracles in me

- I have seeds of greatness inside of me
- I use what I have, and God multiplies it
- I am equipped for greatness

Being a woman is all about bringing a special spark and a sense of mystery with you wherever you go! This can be achieved effortlessly by just being playful, joyful, positive, and light. Activate and allow your playful side to be seen.

As a woman, your feminine energy is always there even if you can't feel it. It just needs to be reawakened. It's an energy that will make you intuitive, compassionate, creative, sensitive, receptive, tender, kind, radiant, nurturing, and – most importantly – unstoppable!

You are A Powerful Woman!

You are a woman, with a *wealth* mindset, because you practice the following:

W- Write Down What You Want

E- Envision Your Future

A-Affirm Your Desire

L- Listen to Your Inner Voice

T- Take Action and Transform

H- Hold the Vision

Today! You have been Activated! You hold the keys to create the life you want. It's Time to dominate and walk in Greatness! You are a masterpiece and one of a kind.

You have what it takes to live a complete, fulfilling and rewarding life.

You were given the power to dominate and conquer whatever you want in this world. 2 timothy 1:7 says, "For the Spirit God gave us does not make us timid, but gives us power, love, and self-discipline."

You hold the vision! Today and Forever, Use your Power! Bring It to Your Reality! You have been Fully Activated!!

Walk, Talk, Breathe, Create... As the Powerful Woman That You Are!

You have been fully charged to fulfill your destiny. Your journey continues!! You have the greatest force in the universe within you. And with it, you will have an amazing life and accomplish amazing things! The powerful source is within you. Use it. Breathe and be present.

Reprogramming: complete.

Press the button within to activate your power, NOW!

POWER WOMAN FACTS

Michelle Obama

Michelle LA Vaughn Robinson Obama (née Robinson; born January 17, 1964) is an American attorney and author who was the First Lady of The United States from 2009 to 2017. She is married to the 44th president of the United States, Barack Obama, and is the first African American First Lady.

Alice Blache'

The history of cinema would be a lot different without Alice Guy-Blaché, who in 1896 became the first ever female film director—at only 23! Guy-Blaché made the first narrative film in history, filmed one of the first close-ups, and invented the concept of filming on location. She made over 1000 films in her lifetime.

Melinda Gates

Gates maintains her position as most powerful woman in philanthropy as co-chair of the Bill and Melinda Gates Foundation.

Founded in 2000, it's the world's largest private charitable foundation with a $40 billion trust endowment.

She's increasingly visible in shaping foundation strategy, solving tough global challenges from education and poverty to contraception and sanitation.

POWERFUL WOMAN
QUOTES

A powerful woman to me is sure of what she wants, knows who she is, and is confident and assertive. She has her own income and business. She stands for what she believes in and gives back to the youth and community. She empowers and uplifts people around her. She has manners and dresses eloquently. She teaches her children. She heals from pain and the past. She speaks wisdom. She's always bettering herself. She forgives herself and finds solutions instead of focusing on the problems. Her spirit is pure, kind, and respectful, yet assertive. She has values and principles. She knows she's the prize, yet she is humble. She makes wise choices and leads by example.

-Jazmin Ave' Henry-Anderson

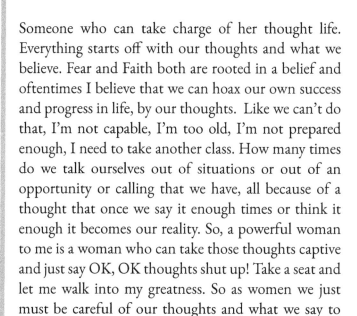

Someone who can take charge of her thought life. Everything starts off with our thoughts and what we believe. Fear and Faith both are rooted in a belief and oftentimes I believe that we can hoax our own success and progress in life, by our thoughts. Like we can't do that, I'm not capable, I'm too old, I'm not prepared enough, I need to take another class. How many times do we talk ourselves out of situations or out of an opportunity or calling that we have, all because of a thought that once we say it enough times or think it enough it becomes our reality. So, a powerful woman to me is a woman who can take those thoughts captive and just say OK, OK thoughts shut up! Take a seat and let me walk into my greatness. So as women we just must be careful of our thoughts and what we say to ourselves. One of the most powerful things in the universe is what we say to ourselves about ourselves. The difference between an average woman and a successful woman is her thought life.

-Clerenda McGrady

"A powerful woman is one who boldly understands that faith and fear cannot co-exist and so she unapologetically views "no" as an opportunity to do it better, to have better and to create something even more amazing."

April Spencer, M. D
CEO, Owner of Just Breast, LLC

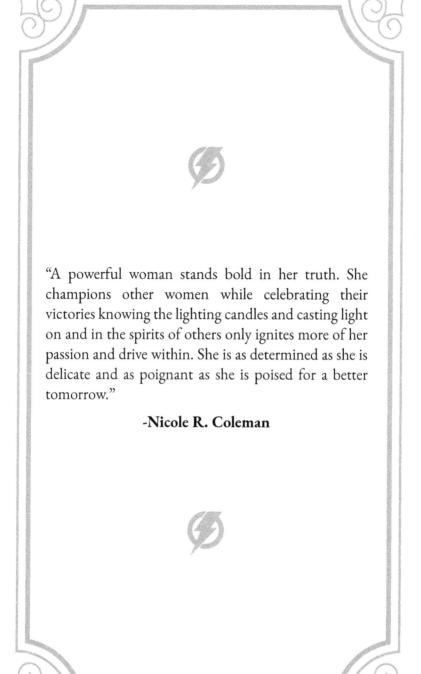

"A powerful woman stands bold in her truth. She champions other women while celebrating their victories knowing the lighting candles and casting light on and in the spirits of others only ignites more of her passion and drive within. She is as determined as she is delicate and as poignant as she is poised for a better tomorrow."

-Nicole R. Coleman

"A powerful woman... Is courageous, confident, resourceful, creative, patient, optimistic, focused, determined, tenacious, persistent, faith filled, fearfully and wonderfully made," Psalm 139:14b, KJV she's valuable and fears the lord.

She's one that has incubated the lessons taught and observed. Then processed and refined the lessons learned, exquisitely found ways to utilize them in various areas to produce their unique flavor; in gifts, talents and promises of purpose through prayer.

Whereas nothing...that has been experienced or observed are lost, but are fuel even building blocks for creating what is imagined or dreamed. The thought, "you can do it knowing nothing is wasted." She uses what's in her hand; what is available, to accomplish her goal. These elements together are the power force that drives her in the direction of her faith, "I can do all things through Christ that strengthens me." Philippians 4:13, KJV. She's relentless in her pursuit of purpose with passion. She trusts in the Lord with all her heart, leans not to her own understanding, but in all her ways acknowledges him (God) and He will direct her path." Proverbs 3;5-6, KJV A powerful woman is kind, courteous and one that will, get it done, no matter the challenge or time... She will succeed! MDB

-Mary English

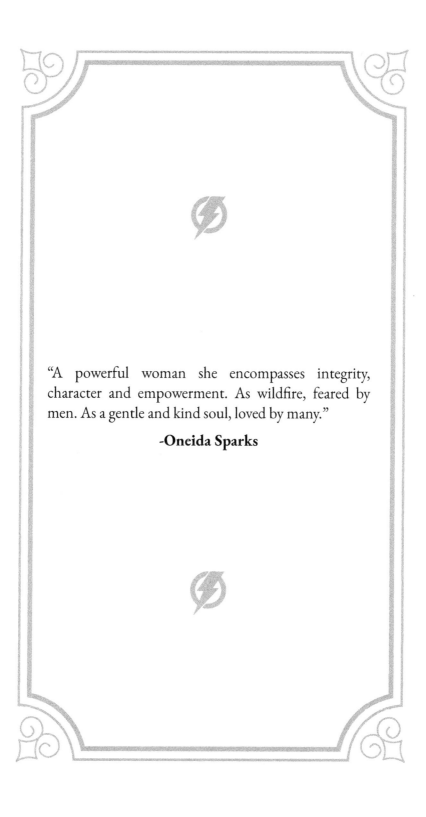

"A powerful woman she encompasses integrity, character and empowerment. As wildfire, feared by men. As a gentle and kind soul, loved by many."

-Oneida Sparks

"Pays it forward, we didn't get here on our own. Someone helped up along the way. It's our duty once women get to a certain plateau or certain rank, that will pull others up. That's what life is all about. At the end of the day if it wasn't for other people. We stand on the shoulder of Giants. No one makes it on their own. A powerful woman is a humble woman. I truly believe that everything here today can be gone tomorrow. So, to be mindful not to put too much into money, too much into fame all those things are fleeting. Need to make sure you have something strong [and] solid that you can stand on. Have a solid foundation. Everything else can be here today and gone tomorrow and always make your bed. When you start with those small things it can end with big results.

-Danielle Hughes

"A woman who despite her inadequacy, despite her insecurities, despite her flaws she still feels confident from within. A powerful woman is a woman who can progress through triumph through her trials and realize that failures don't define her but that she might make mistakes but that's okay because that's a part of her journey that she's on to become the best version of who God has created her to be. I think she's also a woman who celebrates vulnerability and who understands that it's okay to cry to have down moments and it's okay to have failure. Moments in life but that's going to make me who I am in the long term that's going to build my character, my perseverance so that I can become the woman that God has created me to be."

-Loretta Forbes

Humility and wisdom, because as a woman as you grow from a little girl, you grow up you have so many dreams. Especially in a lot of women's lives. Mostly learn growing, most of the things are self-taught because your mother can not teach you what they don't know. So, there's a gap. We can't blame them because they don't know. So, you grow up teaching yourself on this journey and you make a lot of mistakes and then you go back again. It's not bad because you have learned from your mistakes and that makes us become better parents. Now we prepare our children well. To make sure they do not make the mistakes that we made growing up. To learn from a mistake, you must be humbled enough to listen. Then pray for wisdom. Wisdom is in us. That's why God has given us the instinct heart. Women it's a gift from God that we have instinct, you must be open enough for God to show you the wisdom. Because women see what men cannot see. So, if you don't have wisdom you pray for it. I always tell God to give me this wisdom, Holy Spirit, to lead me to know what I am supposed to do in a situation. As long as you put God in the center of your life everything will fall into place.

-Mercy Kaimbah

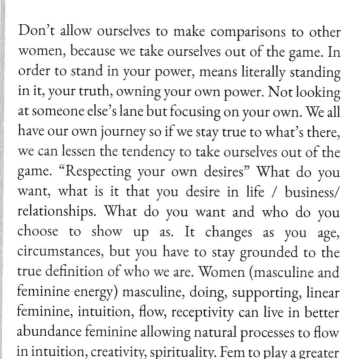

Don't allow ourselves to make comparisons to other women, because we take ourselves out of the game. In order to stand in your power, means literally standing in it, your truth, owning your own power. Not looking at someone else's lane but focusing on your own. We all have our own journey so if we stay true to what's there, we can lessen the tendency to take ourselves out of the game. "Respecting your own desires" What do you want, what is it that you desire in life / business/ relationships. What do you want and who do you choose to show up as. It changes as you age, circumstances, but you have to stay grounded to the true definition of who we are. Women (masculine and feminine energy) masculine, doing, supporting, linear feminine, intuition, flow, receptivity can live in better abundance feminine allowing natural processes to flow in intuition, creativity, spirituality. Fem to play a greater role. In service to our greater self in success.

-Darieth Chisolm

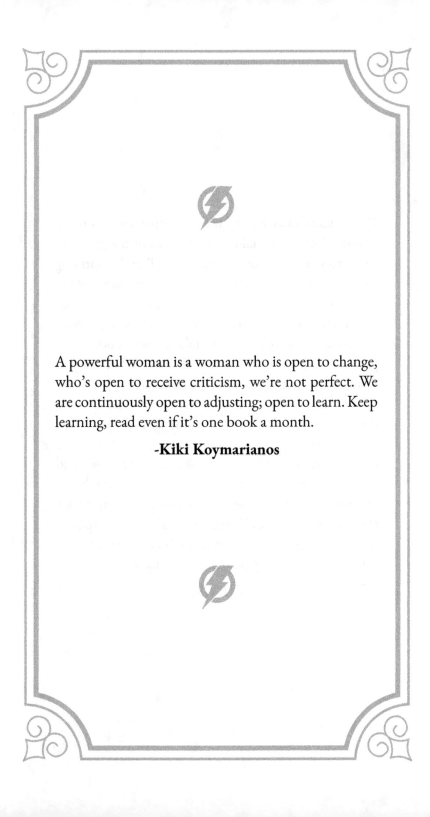

A powerful woman is a woman who is open to change, who's open to receive criticism, we're not perfect. We are continuously open to adjusting; open to learn. Keep learning, read even if it's one book a month.

-Kiki Koymarianos

I think all women are powerful, what society has done is put certain people to highlight. Giving voice to other women, creating a platform and place for other women. To have a voice that oftentimes we could not see. That can say. I don't have to occupy all the oxygen, who sees what others are doing in the community business. Also, someone that is so secure in themselves. That we don't talk, but we walk the walk. Women will say that they want others at the table, but they don't live that, to live that you really have to be in-tuned with your conscience. Also having the confidence to know that if I bring someone to the table, that she might have talents that I don't. That might be appealing to other people, she might rise very high. Very quickly, maybe quicker than me and I have to be confident in myself to know that that's her space and it was for her and to be okay with that. The reason you have to have a lot of confidence and security within herself is because oftentimes people get resentful and we say I'm the one that brought you to the table. You should have told them no, that they should have come to me. Which No! What you should have done was say that they called me, and I want to thank you for creating that opportunity for me and I will remind them that the reason I am here is because of you. When we can start doing that is an authentic way, we will see phenomenal change in the black community.

-Lena Kennedy

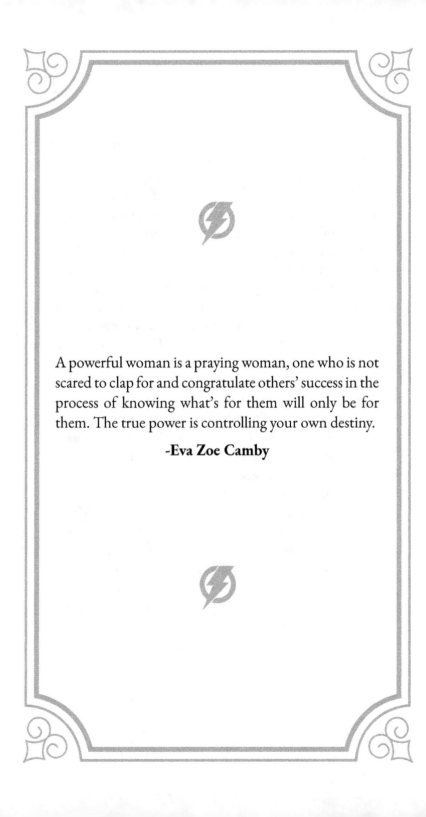

A powerful woman is a praying woman, one who is not scared to clap for and congratulate others' success in the process of knowing what's for them will only be for them. The true power is controlling your own destiny.

-Eva Zoe Camby

"A woman of God who knows her worth. A woman who is sure of herself and is mentally, physically and most important spiritually in tune with her true self. She never settles despite the critics and naysayers and she handled life with compassion. To me power is calculated by how we treat ourselves and others whether it be in our family or communities. Oftentimes people mistake power for political gain, money, or popularity but I believe it is in our character in which the real power lies."

-Courtney Robinson

Being A powerful woman means taking all life hard knocks dead on, looking at them squarely and figuring out a solution never taking the shortcuts or easy ways out. The old adage "what doesn't kill you makes you stronger" is all true! Remember: true power lies in your inner strength, your womanly wisdom and the resilience to know your beauty lies in your ability to persevere no matter what.

-Julie O. Griffith
CEO, Griffith Public Relations
Founder, Champagne & Melanin TM

A powerful woman is self-assured, knows who she is and what she wants and how to get it. She's very influential to others' fearless perseveres and takes the bull [by] the horns all the while, making it look effortless.

-Dr. Tray Andrews, D.C

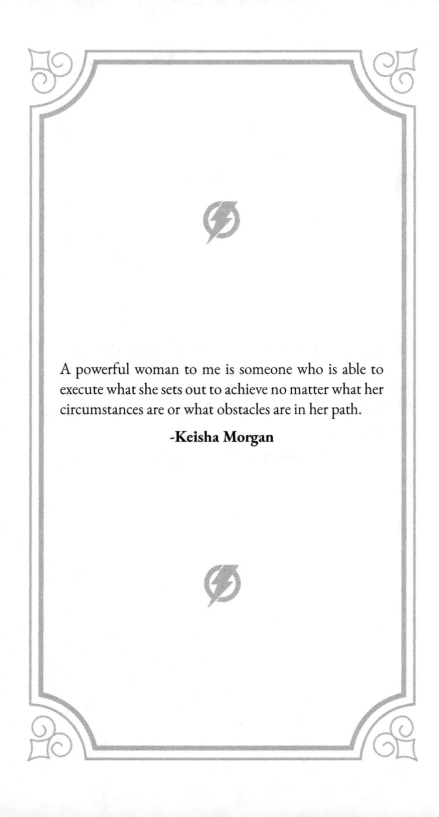

A powerful woman to me is someone who is able to execute what she sets out to achieve no matter what her circumstances are or what obstacles are in her path.

-Keisha Morgan

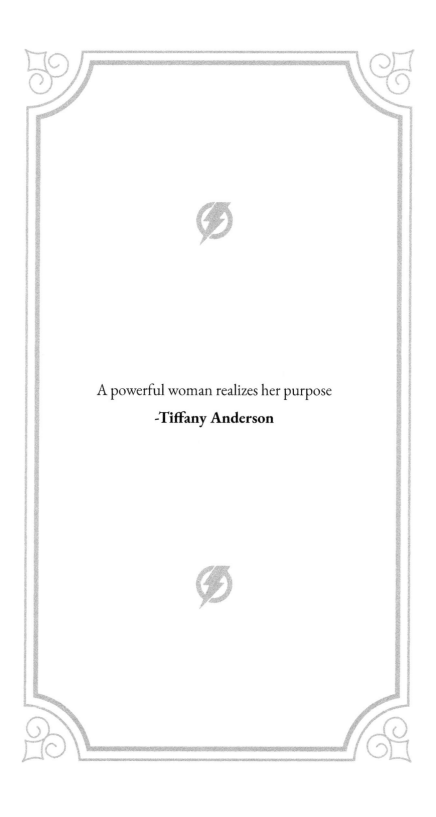

A powerful woman realizes her purpose

-Tiffany Anderson

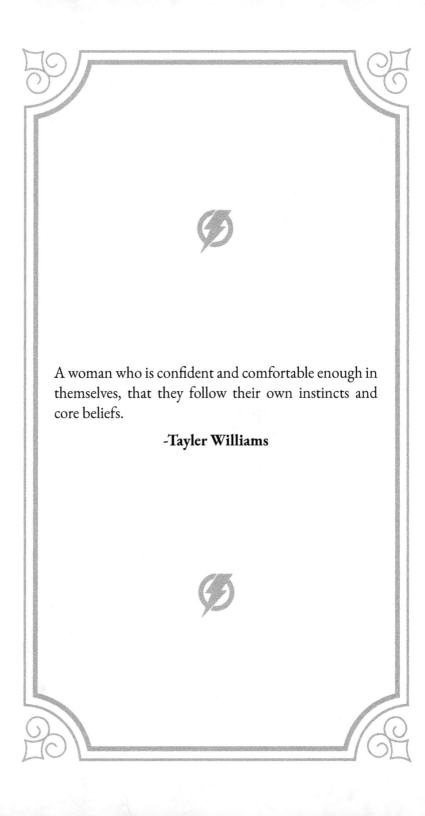

A woman who is confident and comfortable enough in themselves, that they follow their own instincts and core beliefs.

-Tayler Williams

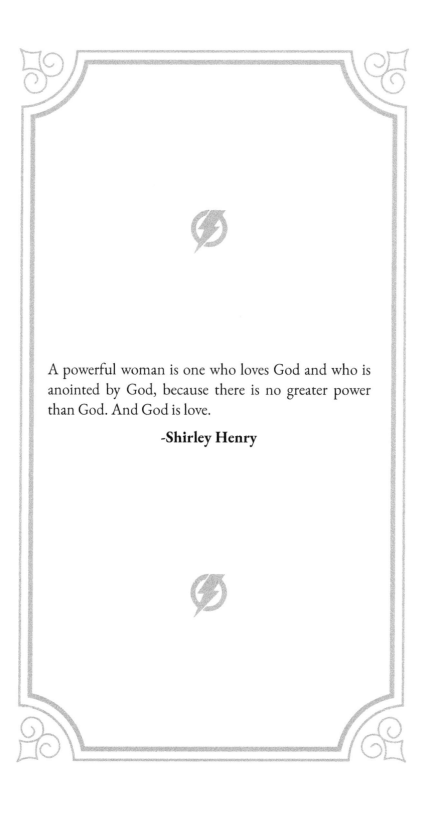

A powerful woman is one who loves God and who is anointed by God, because there is no greater power than God. And God is love.

-Shirley Henry

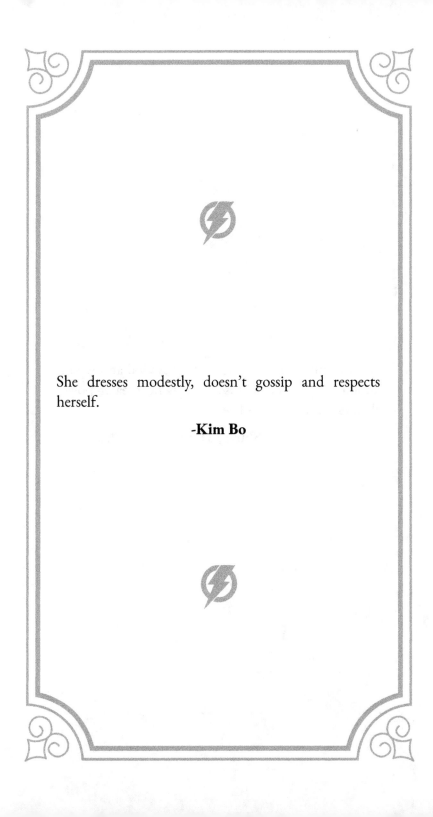

She dresses modestly, doesn't gossip and respects herself.

-Kim Bo

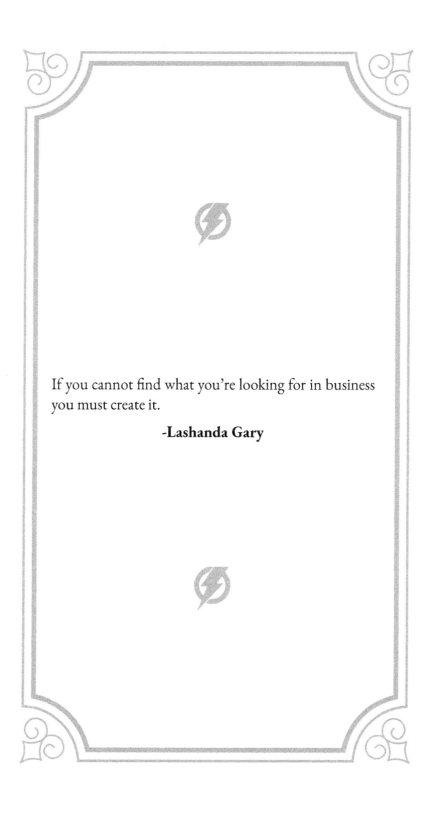

If you cannot find what you're looking for in business you must create it.

-Lashanda Gary

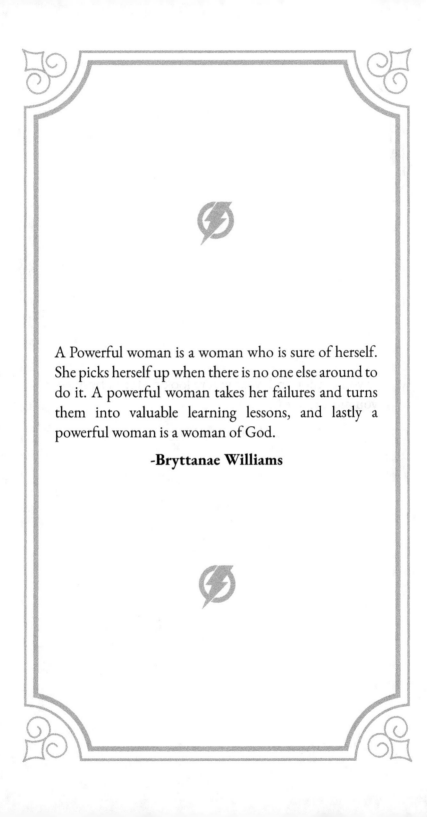

A Powerful woman is a woman who is sure of herself. She picks herself up when there is no one else around to do it. A powerful woman takes her failures and turns them into valuable learning lessons, and lastly a powerful woman is a woman of God.

-Bryttanae Williams

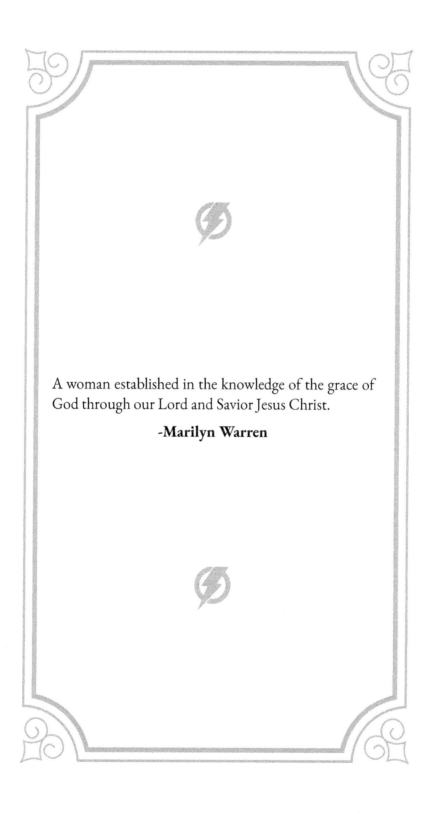

A woman established in the knowledge of the grace of God through our Lord and Savior Jesus Christ.

-Marilyn Warren

1. She understands her lane, she's not trying to be anybody else, but herself. She's clear and uncompromising.

2. She doesn't dim her light, some people will try to tell you you're bright or too much, but you tell them I am "Too Much" for you. Hello! You're not everything to everybody but you are someone to somebody so when you're clear about that, you're not worried about everyone else.

3. Let People have their opinion, that's their business. You be who you're supposed to be.

4. When all of you, who you're purposed to be and your light is on, you're going to shine really bright and for the people who can't stand it, hand them a pair of shades. You just keep being who you are! Right!

5. Be clear on who you are and what your brand is.

6. Be uncompromising about it.

7. Be willing to do whatever it takes and be unapologetic about it.

-Nicole Roberts Jones

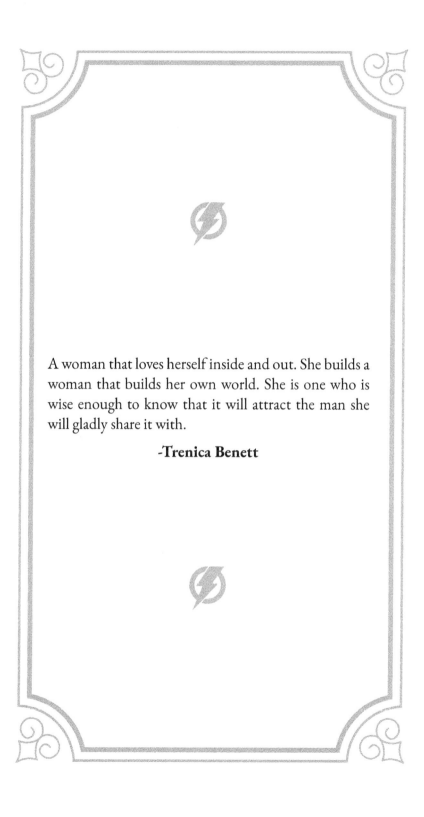

A woman that loves herself inside and out. She builds a woman that builds her own world. She is one who is wise enough to know that it will attract the man she will gladly share it with.

-Trenica Benett

Ephesians 6:10-17 "In conclusion, be strong in the Lord [draw your strength from Him and be empowered through your union with Him] and in the power of His [boundless] might. Put on the full armor of God [for His precepts are like the splendid armor of a heavily armed soldier], so that you may be able to [successfully] stand up against all the schemes and the strategies and the deceits of the devil. For our struggle is not against flesh and blood [contending only with physical opponents], but against the rulers, against the powers, against the world forces of this [present] darkness, against the spiritual forces of wickedness in the heavenly (supernatural) places. Therefore, put on the complete armor of God, so that you will be able to [successfully] resist and stand your ground in the evil day [of danger], and having done everything [that the crisis demands], to stand firm [in your place, fully prepared, immovable, victorious]. So, stand firm and hold your ground, having tightened the wide band of truth (personal integrity, moral courage) around your waist and having put on the breastplate of righteousness (an upright heart), and having strapped on your feet the gospel of peace in preparation [to face the enemy with firm-footed stability and the readiness produced by the good news]. Above all, lift up the [protective] shield of faith with which you can extinguish all the flaming arrows of the evil one. And take the helmet of salvation, and the sword of the Spirit, which is the Word of God." I look at being a powerful woman in a spiritual sense because God is a spirit. We fall short daily and are weak without God's given strength and we must seek him for I can do all things through Christ, who gives me strength. Philippians 4:13

-Nicko English

What makes a woman powerful is the faith that she wears. She could go through so much pain in her lifetime but yet when you look at her she seems like she's never been through anything, it's almost like she seems so happy and so beautiful. Then she will only let you see what she allows you to see, you wouldn't be able to see her coming or understand her movement is always catching you off guard and her love is so deep. Like a dark deep blue ocean that doesn't have an ending to it. She is so strong that even when a life is taken from her, she can still move forward. She is so powerful that you can feel her vibrate through her pictures, videos even when she smiles.

-Racanee Brown

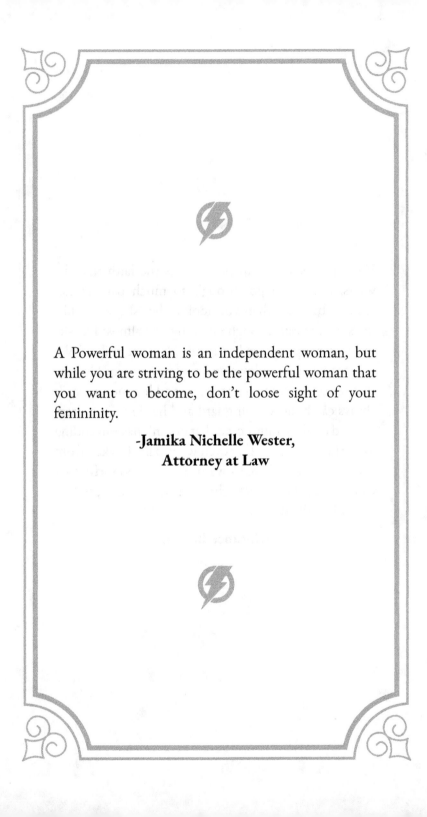

A Powerful woman is an independent woman, but while you are striving to be the powerful woman that you want to become, don't loose sight of your femininity.

-Jamika Nichelle Wester,
Attorney at Law

ACKNOWLEDGEMENTS:

I want to thank God for giving me the vision to create this book and the strength and resources for completing this beautiful masterpiece. It has been a beautiful experience. I have learned and gained so much knowledge on this journey. I pray that women walk away feeling more empowered and uplifted in their journey to be their greatest self.

I am truly thankful for everyone who has helped with putting this book together, from the graphics, cover photo, editing, layout, to the whole team. Thank you!

To All the beautiful women who shared their quotes on what a powerful woman is, thank you for adding value to the book with your words. I truly appreciate everyone's time and dedication.

I want to thank my son, Princetin, for being patient and supportive on all the days he had to be quiet or understanding when I needed to focus so I could write. I am so blessed to have the Most Amazing Child in the world. You light up my life every day and add so much more value and meaning to it. Being your mother has inspired me to be my best and give you the best. I learn from you everyday whether you know it or not. A lot of my creative endeavors are to make sure you are a part of shaping a better future. I love you, son.

I also want to thank my friends and family for continuing to support me.

To my Mom (Tiffany), thanks for always being there and loving me and supporting me when I need you. To my Dad (Leonard), thanks for loving me and supporting me. To My Grandmommy (Jewel), thank you for being my best friend and loving me and supporting me. I am truly blessed to have an amazing family.

To My Amazing Siblings, (I Am the oldest out of 7), Janae, Jasily, Westley, Joy, Leila & Leighton. May you all continue to be empowered to be your best and use your power for good. I love you all and pray that all your dreams will become your reality.

To Quentin, you being a great father allows me the time to do the great things I need to do in the world.

To Sharon Jenkins, thank you for everything you do. You truly have shown me a lot about being an author from attending events to writing and helping me stay focused. Thank you for letting God use you.

It's very rarely that you can find someone who's an open book and mentors someone to greatness, thank you Calvin for your invaluable support and your uplifting words every day.

Grady Carter, thank you for the amazing photos-- the cover photo came out perfect.

Kenny, thank you for your support with the behind-the-scenes graphics and input.

Again, I am truly thankful for everyone who has helped put this book together. Thank you McWriting Services.

To the readers, I pray that you walk away feeling empowered and powerful. You hold the keys to your future.

ABOUT THE AUTHOR

JAZMIN AVE' ANDERSON is an American radio television personality, on a mission to connect people with the world inside and outside of themselves. She has spent 10 years hosting events as well as radio & television shows from coast to coast. Today through radio, TV, podcasting & social media, Jazmin is connecting people with spiritualism that's relevant and beneficial to their lives. She is a woman with a passion for people and the media. She is an outgoing, down to earth, loving, creative, and intelligent human being. Jazmin was birthed into the world, in Long Beach, California. She was raised in the city of Los Angeles and San Fernando Valley. Her Sophomore year in high school is where she discovered that she wanted to be a journalist. She was fascinated by other people's stories and how they lived their everyday lives. She has a way of speaking and getting the attention of her viewing and listening audience. Jazmin moved to Houston, Texas, at 17, where she started her career in the media. She worked on the set of the Deborah Duncan Show, Good Morning

Houston in 2010. From there she joined a Toastmasters club to improve her speaking ability. She later co-hosted The Vangundy Show in 2013. Jazmin also co-hosted a gospel event with Marcus D. Wiley in the same year. Improving and evolving as a young woman, she gained more knowledge in her field. She went to London for a "Sports Management Worldwide" Conference, where she met former players and learned the business side of media in 2014. She also attended the "Prime Time" Sports Management Conference in Toronto, Canada.

In September 2014, Jazmin worked with Yahoo Radio Sports and ESPN where she gained experiences in both radio and television. She has always been excited about and receptive to open opportunities to improve herself and increase her knowledge in the media industry. It has opened numerous doors for her. From-2015-2020, Jazmin has done sound bite coverage on Radio Row for the

Super Bowl. She has interviewed celebrities like Mathew Knowles, Yolanda Adams, Lisa Raye, Jaheim, Carl Payne, Eric Bennett, DeeRay Davis, and Lil Flip just to name a few.

Jazmin has very diverse interview skills and recently interviewed several NBA players, as well as getting the inside scoop on the players from the Rockets Locker Room. She has interviewed the 28-0 Boxing Champion Jermel Charlo as well as other athletes.

Jazmin Anderson has been a freelance reporter who has worked with Channel ATV on Award Shows and Mega conferences. She has traveled state to state getting coverage with the team. She has also worked with 953jamz.com hosting a show called Fresh Start Sunday motivating her listeners with words of wisdom, success, & motivational clips. Another Media outlet Jazmin has worked with is KYND (knowledge you need daily) Radio 1520am. She is always a part of a team where talk inspires change. In 2015 Jazmin started her own media company. She is the CEO/ Founder of JTV ONE global television. (www.jtvone.com)

Where she writes, produce, and interviews a new guest every week to share their story on how they have become successful as well as overcoming their obstacles. She strives to encourage and uplift people through everything she does.

In August 2017, Jazmin Anderson published her first book "Live Fully" Ten Golden Rules to Live a Rich Life.

In 2019, Jazmin received an award from Mayor Yolanda Ford for A Salute of Excellence In helping Make A difference. She has also been recognized by Councilmember Ellen R. Cohen for her service to Houston and being a part of Girls Who Brunch Tour. In October 2020, she was an "Honoree" as a Media Personality from Broadcast Houston. She is continuing to use her voice to enlighten & inform people. She also goes out into the community to feed the homeless and is always volunteering for charities and events that better mankind.

Jazmin Anderson has interviewed people in sports, entertainment, fashion, religion, and politics. Her love for people and empowering others in a positive way will take her a long way. She is a beautiful person inside and out, with an ambition to intentionally share her influence for good in the world of media.

REFERENCES

Ch.2   Gods Voice Vs. Other Voices: How can you tell the difference? www.supernatuaraldiscernment.com

Ch.3   Virtuous Woman (Bible Verse) "The Woman's Study Bible, King James Version Copyright 2012 by Thomas Nelson, Inc.

Ch.5   Principle definition- Merriam Webster dictionary

Ch.6   Intuition definition- dictionary.com